Nyerere Remembered

Lawrence E.K. Lupalo

Nyerere Remembered

First Edition

ISBN-13: 978-1539471608
ISBN-10: 1539471608

CreateSpace
Scotts Valley, California, USA

Mwalimu Julius Nyerere

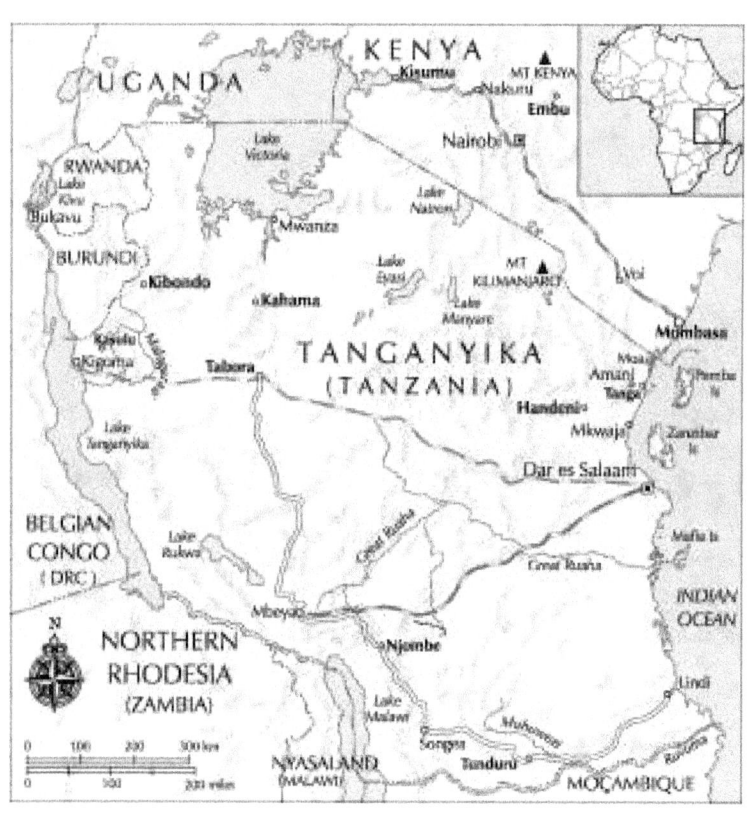

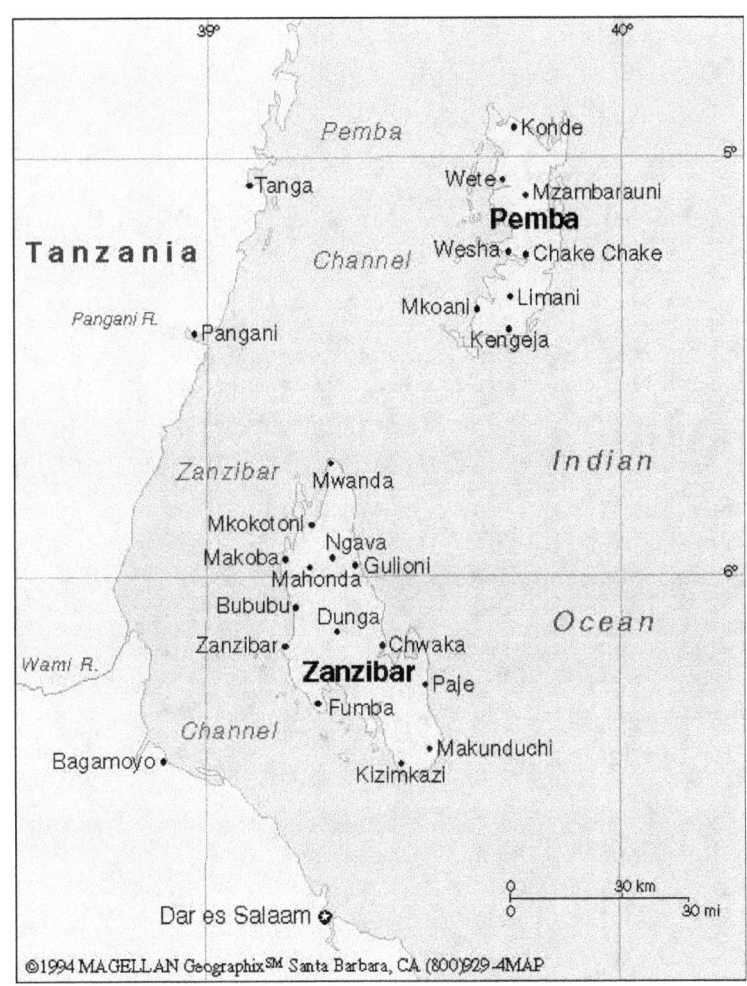

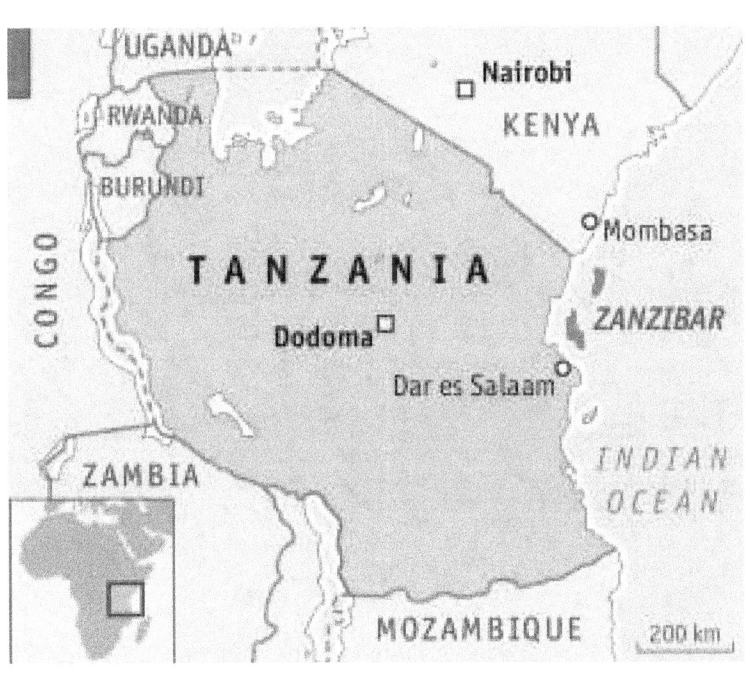

8

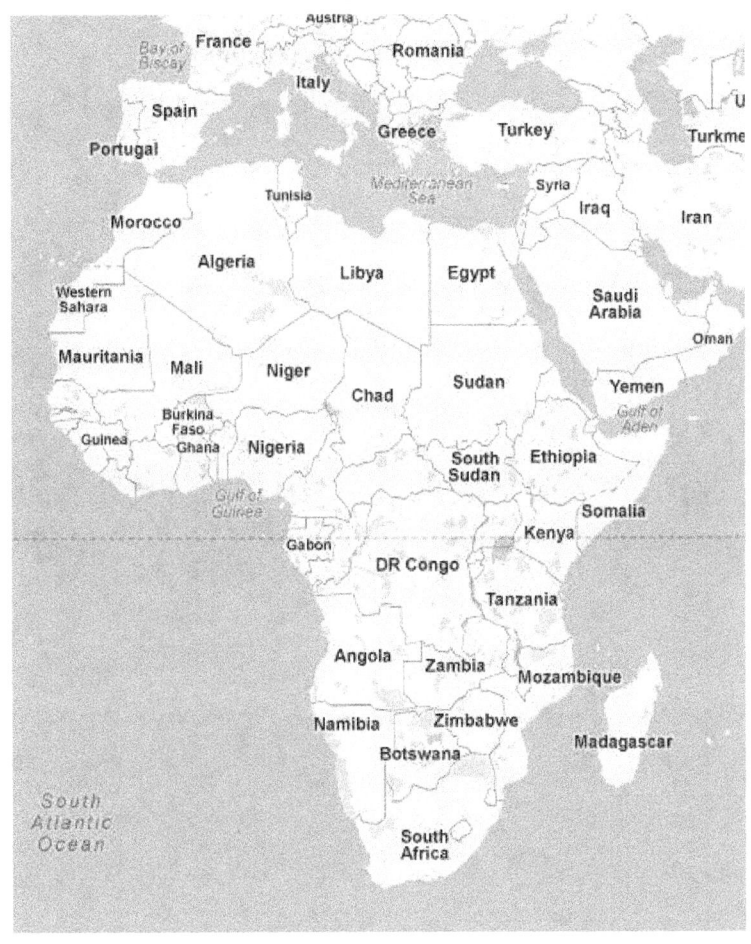

Introduction

THIS WORK looks at Julius Nyerere, the first president of Tanganyika – later Tanzania – from different perspectives as a leader who played the most important role in shaping the destiny of his country after it won independence from Britain on 9 December 1961.

He also helped shape the destiny of his continent because of the leading role he played in the liberation struggle in the countries of southern Africa which were still under white minority rule.

The work also looks at Nyerere simply as a person whose values and commitment to the wellbeing of others thrust him into a position of leadership since his student days when he was chosen to be a prefect in secondary school and refused to be granted special privileges over his fellow students simply because he was one of their leaders.

It was those same values and convictions which also made him stand out among other African leaders and earned him the title, "The conscience of Africa."

Even other people who were not Africans acknowledged his status as a moral leader who upheld high principles. As *Newsweek* stated when he died, "The world has lost a man of principle," in spite of the fact that it was highly critical of his economic policies.

The fact that many people, including world leaders, did not agree with his policies and some of the major decisions he made affecting the wellbeing of Africa in general, did not in any way diminish his stature as man of conscience, a rare attribute among politicians; it only enhanced his status as a highly respected leader on the global stage when they showered praise on him for being highly ethical, committed, and selfless.

The opinions of those who disagreed with him on a number of issues constitute a substantial part of this book for one simple reason. Had I compiled the opinions of those who agreed with him on virtually everything, the work would clearly have been biased towards him and would have lost credibility.

Coming from his critics, the wide range of opinions from different perspectives and on a number of different subjects contained in this book can be considered to be an objective assessment of what kind of person and leader Nyerere was. They are not his praise singers. And therein lies the strength of this work, in spite of its shortcomings as a work of a mere mortal.

Lawrence E.K. Lupalo
Dar es Salaam, Tanzania
10 October 2016

Nyerere Remembered

JULIUS NYERERE was one of the most prominent and most influential leaders Africa has ever produced. He was also a major Third World leader.

He was also considered to be a world leader, not just an African leader. Even many of his critics accorded him that status.

He was not an ordinary leader. He was highly respected around the world because of the kind of leadership he provided. He was a man of principle and high moral integrity who never wavered when he took a stand on vital issues affecting the wellbeing of Africa. That is why he came to be acknowledged as "The conscience of Africa." His fellow African leaders also nicknamed him "OAU's minister of foreign affairs."

He even spoke on behalf of other African leaders when he visited other countries after stepping down as president of Tanzania. As he himself said, whenever he travelled outside Africa, he had to explain what was going on in Rwanda, Liberia, Somalia and other African countries. His hosts in Europe, America and other parts of the world expected him to answer questions about other African countries because he was an African. His identity as a

Tanzanian was eclipsed by his identity as an African. As he stated before the South African parliament in Cape Town on 16 October 1997 in a speech that was informal and delivered in a conversational tone and style:

"Here I am, president, former president of my country, no problem in Tanzania, we have never had these problems that they have — but I am an African and they see me and they ask me (about) the problems of Rwanda, but I don't come from Rwanda — (and they answer) 'But you come from Africa.' But I don't meet everybody, I don't meet an Englishman somewhere, eh, if Blair were to come to Dar es Salaam, I wouldn't ask him what is happening in Bosnia; it never occurs to me — I should ask Blair, 'What is happening to you Europeans?' because of what is happening there (in Bosnia). If President Kohl was to come from somewhere, I don't ask him, 'What is happening in Chechnya?' Kohl could say, 'Why are you asking me anything about Chechnya, I don't know what is happening in Chechnya.' But this not true about Africa....

Of course I am a Tanzanian, but what is this Tanzania? Why should these Europeans see me as a Tanzanian — what is Tanzania? This is something we tried to create in my lifetime. I built Tanzania — so what is this Tanzania? The Europeans are right, North Americans are right to look at me as an African."

He articulated the same position a few months before, in March 1997, in his speech in Accra on the 40th anniversary of Ghana's independence:

"We are all Africans trying very hard to be Ghanaians or Tanzanians. Fortunately for Africa, we have not been completely successful.

The outside world hardly recognises our Ghanaianness or Tanzanian-ness. What the outside world recognises about us is our Africanness....

When I travel outside Africa, the description of me as a former president of Tanzania is a fleeting affair. It does not stick. Apart from the ignorant who sometimes asked me whether Tanzania was in Johannesburg, even to those who knew better, what stuck in the minds of my hosts was the fact of my African-ness.

So I had to answer questions about the atrocities of the Amins and Bokassas of Africa. Mrs [Indira] Ghandi [the former Indian prime minister] did not have to answer questions about the atrocities of the Marcoses of Asia. Nor does Fidel Castro have to answer questions about the atrocities of the Somozas of Latin America.

But when I travel or meet foreigners, I have to answer questions about Somalia, Liberia, Rwanda, Burundi and Zaire, as in the past I used to answer questions about Mozambique, Angola, Zimbabwe, Namibia or South Africa.

And the way I was perceived is the way most of my fellow heads of state were perceived. And that is the way you [the people of Africa] are all being perceived. So accepting the fact that we are Africans, gives you a much more worthwhile challenge than the current desperate attempts to fossilise Africa into the wounds inflicted upon it by the vultures of imperialism. Do not be proud of your shame. Reject the return to the tribe, there is richness of culture out there which we must do everything we can to preserve and share.

But it is utter madness to think that if these artificial, unviable states which we are trying to create are broken up into tribal components and we turn those into nation-states we might save ourselves. That kind of political and social atavism spells catastrophe for Africa. It would be the end of any kind of genuine development for Africa. It would fossilise Africa into a worse state than the one in which we are."

During his leadership, Nyerere succeeded in building

one of the most united and most stable countries in Africa and in the entire world. Tribalism is virtually non-existent in Tanzania because of the kind of leadership he provided. Tanzanians see themselves as one people, simply as Tanzanians and as Africans unlike their brethren in most part of the continent where tribalism thrives and threatens national unity.

Nyerere transformed a former colony, once ruled by Germany and then Britain, into a model of stability and racial harmony unheard of in many parts of the world. And even though he had profound political and ideological differences with Western leaders whose nations ruled Africa during the colonial era and are still trying to dominate Africa, those differences did not diminish his stature – even in the West – as a highly principled leader just as the differences Mao had with the West did not in anyway diminish his stature as a great leader in spite of the mistakes he made. Great leaders always make big mistakes which demonstrate that they are mere mortals like the rest of us in spite of their greatness.

China would not be what it is today had it not been for the foundation laid by Mao.

Ghana would not be what it is today had it not been for Nkrumah – he laid the foundation for modern Ghana – and achieved a lot in less than 10 years he was prime minister and president. He was prime minister for three years and president for almost six years before he was overthrown in February 1966 in a military coup engineered by the United States and Britain together with France and West Germany. According to declassified documents, the leaders of those countries met at the White House in Washington, D.C., a number of times to formulate plans, including a military coup, on how to get rid of Nkrumah.

Every successive government in Ghana has built on the foundation laid by Nkrumah and has acknowledged its indebtedness to him.

And Tanzania would not be what it is today had it not

16

been for the foundation laid by Nyerere.

It is worth remembering that Western leaders who were highly critical of Nyerere's policies – including his uncompromising stand against imperial domination of Africa and other parts of the Third World by the West and other powers – are the same people who also had very high regard for him because of his leadership qualities and his stature as a world leader.

One of the Western leaders who acknowledged that Nyerere was a world leader was President Jimmy Carter of the United States of America.

That is a very high compliment for a leader of a poor, Third World country like Tanzania. But that was Nyerere. When he died, a report in *The Washington Post* stated that during Nyerere's leadership, Tanzania was one of the top 25 countries in the world. It punched above its weight, and came to be acknowledged as a leading country in the international arena, because of Nyerere.

Professor Ali Mazrui, a towering intellectual of international standing and one of the best Africa has ever produced, articulated the same position in terms of Nyerere's achievements, also contending that Nyerere did not get the credit he deserved as a great nation builder:

"Nyerere's policies of nation-building amount to a case of Unsung Heroism. With wise and strong leadership, and with brilliant policies of cultural integration, he took one of the poorest countries in the world and made it a proud leader in African affairs and an active member of the global community." (Ali A. Mazrui, "Nyerere and I," in *Voices*, Africa Resource Center, October 1999: Professor Ali Mazrui writes a memorial tribute on the special bonds between him and the late Mwalimu Julius Nyerere, one of Africa's few great statesmen.)

Tanzania was held in high esteem when Nyerere was in power. That is no longer the case. That is because no leader of comparable moral stature has led Tanzania since his departure. The only one who may have followed in his footsteps in terms of commitment to the wellbeing of the masses and fighting corruption and elitism is the fifth president, John Magufuli. But he does not have the moral authority and the political base Nyerere had to exert strong influence on the country as a whole and shape its destiny.

That is in sharp contrast with the past, what we were as a nation, under the leadership of Nyerere.

Nyerere

American ambassadors who knew Nyerere and who were accredited to Tanzania during his presidency acknowledged that he was a world leader, not just a Tanzanian or an African leader. They also said he was a selfless leader who was fully committed to the wellbeing of his people. They also admitted that he was a man of enormous intellect.

Some of them are quoted by Godfrey Mwakikagile in his book, *Why Tanganyika united with Zanzibar to form Tanzania*. As he states:

"Deputy American ambassador Robert Hennemeyer who was in Tanganyika, later Tanzania, from 1961 – 1964, described President Nyerere as 'a great political theorist,...a charismatic figure,...a great leader of his people. **I don't believe for a moment** that he meant anything but to do the best he could for the wellbeing of his people....He had an enormous amount of influence with other black African leaders. He was so revered as the great father....**Clearly he was a world leader,** not just an African leader.'

Ambassador Claude G. Ross described Nyerere as a leader who was 'full of good intentions and the epitome of integrity....I don't think any kind of financial scandal was ever attached to him....He was a very interesting man, very articulate, you know, and had a better education. He'd gone to Edinburgh and had advanced training, not a doctorate, but advanced training.'

Ambassador John H. Burns had the following to say about Nyerere:

'The country had a President, the remarkable Julius Nyerere, unique---then and ever since in Africa...a highly intelligent and cultivated president....He, himself, lived very simply and insisted that members of his government do likewise.

I have rarely known anyone more dedicated to what he saw as his purpose in life. I once said that the song 'The Impossible Dream' could have been written for him.

He was a remarkably educated and cultured man, a graduate of the University of Edinburgh. One of his hobbies was translating Shakespeare into Swahili and one or two of them --Julius Caesar was one-- were performed at the University of Dar es Salaam, an institution in which Nyerere, not surprisingly, took great interest.....

We couldn't attract much attention from Washington for Nyerere. He was regarded by certain influential circles of the Johnson administration as a dangerous thinker.'

In the words of Ambassador John W. Shirley:

'I enjoyed the fact that during my tenure in Dar es Salaam Julius Nyerere was still President of Tanzania. I found him an interesting and extremely intelligent man. And since South Africa was in turmoil at the time, and because Nyerere was, to say the least, not particularly sympathetic to the policy of constructive engagement, my meetings with him were frequent, animated, sometimes sharp, but never acrimonious. It was as intellectually stimulating to deal with him, as it was to deal with Prime Minister Salim Salim.'

Ambassador W. Beverly Carter described Nyerere in the following terms:

'Julius Nyerere was...one of the early heroes, political heroes, of mine and of many other Africanists....(He) was an extremely popular person....(Other African) countries tended to look to Tanzania for leadership, and Nyerere was never hesitant about offering it and giving it and doing it well. He is probably one of the most principled men I ever met in my life....

I talked earlier about my Government's ambivalence about Tanzania....Nyerere should have been treated more like the world leader that he is and that everyone recognized him to be....Just unheard of for a man of his...Nyerere's worldwide leadership being treated, I felt, as, not as well as other people who didn't come nearly up to his size. It's sort of symptomatic of the problem I had in dealing with my own Government....

You didn't think of (President) Tolbert (of Liberia) as being ... a Kenneth Kaunda or Julius Nyerere. He didn't have that capability, was not an intellectual giant. He did not even have quite the quality that Botswana's Seretse Khama had, who was not a giant intellectually the way I think Nkrumah was or Nyerere is.....

With Nyerere it was the kind of relationship that you have in a dormitory at night when you're engaging in a good debate.'

Ambassador James W. Spain described Nyerere this way:

'Nyerere's rule was relatively benign. I am quite sure he never ordered anybody killed. There were a few people in jail but not many. Some were from Zanzibar, under sentence of death there but kept alive on the mainland....People didn't get killed. They might get relocated under the ujamaa system of farming, but Nyerere never even thought of 'liquidating the kulaks'....

He was a hopeless socialist. Still, he was clearly a very sincere and humane man.

If I did anything useful, it was to convince Washington that Nyerere was not a brutal African dictator and a Communist stooge....I found Nyerere fascinating....I never read a book that he hadn't read. He translated Shakespeare into Kiswahili....I am very fond of Julius Nyerere....

Most Western development aid to Tanzania came from Scandinavia, particularly the Swedes. They liked the intellectual socialist, the benign father of his people who didn't kill or imprison people, while trying to create a new way of life with better prospects....Unlike other parts of Africa, no one was starving or dying of uncontrolled disease in Tanzania.... He was basically a humanist with a keen sense of both tribal traditions and modern politics....

The fact was that Nyerere certainly wasn't on our side, but he wasn't a tool of the Chinese or the Russians either....

I was personally very fond of Nyerere--not necessarily a good thing for a diplomat. He was a very remarkable man and, I think, a very constructive element in the peaceful solutions to the problems of Southern Africa that eventually emerged.'

Ambassador Richard N. Viets said the following about Nyerere:

'At that time in mid-1979, the so-called front-line states in Southern Africa, I think there were five of them...the organization was chaired by Julius Nyerere, the President of Tanzania, a very remarkable gentleman. Nyerere really towered over the other four heads of state and this organization in many respects was a one-man operation.

Because of his long association with the independence movements in East Africa and throughout Southern Africa he was highly respected.

Nyerere is an intellectual of very considerable dimensions, an extraordinarily articulate person. So the leadership of this group was essentially his without any challenge. He was offering almost daily advise to the Zimbabwean leadership on tactics, strategy, etc. in their negotiations with the British and the Americans and the others involved....

I decided I needed to know more about Julius Nyerere than anybody else on the face of the earth.... He is a very shrewd man.

He was...a most remarkable figure in contemporary African political history. I always said, and others who knew him well I think shared this view, that if Nyerere had been born in Western Europe or the Far East or even in North America, he would have been an exceptional figure in public life. He was a superb politician.

He had an acute brain, the memory of an elephant, intellectual horsepower that was second to none.

He was cunning. He could be warm-hearted one moment and cut you off at the legs at the next if it met his political or personal needs. He had, of course, been the principal political figure behind the Tanzanian independence movement in the 1950s....

Nyerere...remains as far as I know the principal translator of Shakespeare from English into Swahili and one of the most gifted orators I have ever heard in English, and a marvelous drafter of the English language....

I can remember listening to him rail hour after hour against the IMF and the prescriptions the IMF was demanding of Tanzania that he argued would send it further into poverty, etc....

Nyerere regime's record is...in the human rights arena when one is talking about imprisonment and torture, or loaded legal shenanigans against opposition, I think his record is remarkably good. If human rights include the right to a job, an education, hospitalization, etc., then you have to give him pretty good marks.'

Ambassador Viets also acknowledged how intelligent Salim Ahmed Salim was:

In the final months of my tour the Foreign Minister of Tanzania was a gentleman named Salim Salim, who nearly became the Secretary General of the United Nations. I think he would have had it not been for George Bush.

Bush remembered Salim Salim as the Tanzanian delegate who came and danced in front of his chair in the General Assembly the day the Chinese were admitted to the United Nations. And Bush never forgot Mr. Salim Salim. I found Salim Salim, who I think is now Secretary General of the OAU, to be a very, very bright, interesting man whose revolutionary zeal had long since cooled.'

Ambassador David C. Miller, a staunch Republican, said the following about Nyerere:

'He was on his way to the Cancun summit, **the only head of government from Africa** among the 13 presidents at Cancun. He was the leader of the frontline states in the negotiations over Resolution 435, which was the Namibian independence resolution passed by the UN. In terms of national power at home, he was at quite a peak. Physically, he was old enough to be wise and young enough to be vigorous. He was a great guy to work with....

Nyerere had been a world leader of the non-aligned movement for a long time. His economic policies were well-known and the impact of his economic policies had been apparent for some period of time. In a nutshell, on the domestic front, Tanzania had succeeded in integrating itself as a political entity.

Bu there was also Julius Nyerere's belief that it was important for every citizen of Tanzania to move forward roughly together economically and to integrate themselves socially and that over a period of time his approach to the economic management of Tanzania would produce a more coherent, unified country than, as he was fond of pointing out, Kenya, his next-door neighbor, which was our favorite country. So, domestically, he had succeeded with a single party approach to governing Tanzania and thought that that had worked well for him...

Wonderful, warm, friendly, smart, honest, brave, humble. He was as great a head of government as Africa has seen as evidenced not by his ability to do the little day-to-day things of running a country but on the big accounts, the most important being his lifestyle, which remained humble throughout his whole time as head of government. Most remarkable, was his retirement from the presidency at a time when he was perfectly capable of going on physically.

Then, of course, he returned to his village upcountry as one of the few heads of government in Africa who behaved the way George Washington behaved here and said, 'We do not need presidents for life in Africa and I don't intend to be one.'

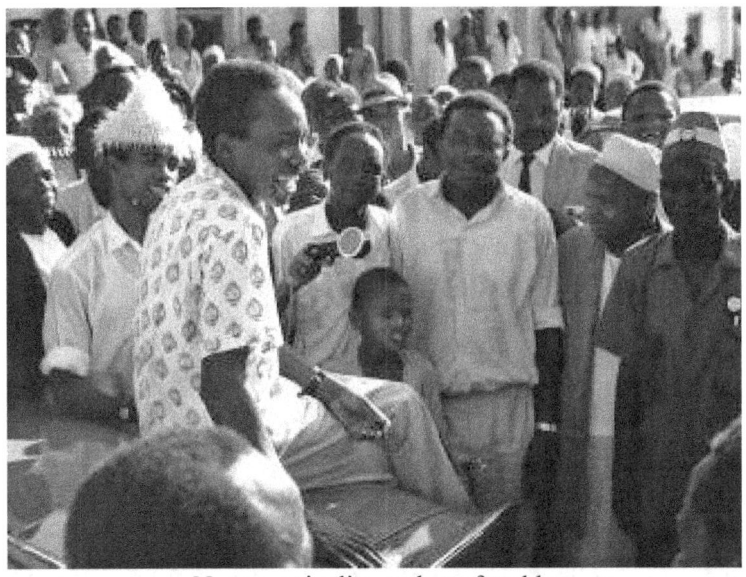

Nyerere mingling and comfortable
with ordinary people in Dar es Salaam

Frankly, he was probably happiest when he was back home in Butiama with his wife and grandchildren in a very humble home. It was hard to get to by vehicle. So, for me, he stands out in stark relief to the failed public leadership in Africa that can be found in almost every country....

Julius Nyerere because of his global leadership - and this is the thing that you have to remember: nobody in their right mind today can tell you who was president of Burundi or Rwanda 20 years ago; Julius was an international author, an international statesman, and used that effectively as a head of government to gain support for Tanzania well beyond either its objective importance or its internal economic performance. To a great degree, that's what a head of government in a developing country ought to be trying to achieve. Julius achieved that.

So, did the economy ever work perfectly? No. Did it achieve what he wanted? Yes, it did. It produced a level economic base that is now producing a solid Tanzanian economy without the disasters that befell Kenya. If Julius were here today sitting with us, he would say, 'I told you, David. Kenya turned into a corrupt mud hole. Tanzania is now slowly taking off the ground with responsible leadership in a country that's socially unified.' I'm happy to make that argument for him....

It was an outstanding diplomatic world simply because of Nyerere's presence and who he was and the importance of having Julius' support when he was head of the Non-Aligned Movement, of having Julius' support when he was running the Frontline States. When Julius Nyerere spoke or traveled, people listened to him. So, countries that were playing in that environment wanted to have a good mission in Dar es Salaam....

He had a position on the world....He was first and foremost an intellectual and an ideologue.... Julius Nyerere was an intellect. He wanted to talk to people about his ideas and what worked and didn't work.'" – (Godfrey Mwakikagile, *Why Tanganyika united with Zanzibar to form Tanzania*, Dar es Salaam, Tanzania: New Africa Press, 2014, pp. 128 – 134, and 430. See also, Godfrey Mwakikagile, *The Union of Tanganyika and Zanzibar: Formation of Tanzania and its Challenges*, New Africa Press, 2016).

The invitation of Nyerere to the Cancun summit, being the only African leader who was invited, is another example which demonstrates the profound respect Western leaders had for Mwalimu as a spokesman for the entire African continent because of his keen understanding of Africa's problems.

Nyerere's keen insights into Africa's problems and of

the entire Third World were also acknowledged by his critics and admirers alike in both ideological camps – East and West. As Professor Gerry Helleiner of the University of Toronto who worked in Tanzania for many years stated not long after Nyerere died:

"It is now 'conventional wisdom' in Washington (even in the IMF, at least in terms of its rhetoric) and in donor capitals that poverty needs to be addressed as a matter of highest priority; that political stability and good governance (notably reduced corruption) are prerequisites for development; and that national ownership of programmes is critical to their success. It has taken them a long time to reach these positions. But Julius Nyerere was espousing them and trying to build practice upon them 30 years ago. His slogan of "socialism and self-reliance", if transmitted today as "equity, honesty and ownership", would win universal assent. He was decades ahead of his time in these matters....

Whatever his other mistakes in the realm of economics, in one area of economic policy Mwalimu was dead right - and, again, ahead of his time. Both in his anguished cry about the IMF in 1981 and in his subsequent work in the South Commission and the South Centre, he steadily maintained the need for fairer international (or global) systems of economic governance, particularly in the financial sphere. It is important to underline his consistent emphasis upon *equity* in global economic governance arrangements....

Nyerere's activities in the international/global sphere included efforts to bolster analysis, both economic and political, to inform those who speak for the developing countries, especially the poorest among them, in international negotiations and organizations. The developing countries are still woefully weakly equipped to deal with the batteries of well-funded economists, lawyers and lobbyists who defend Northern interests in international discussions and the media. He was among those who saw, far ahead of others, that there is ultimately no substitute for one's own technical, professional and institutional strength. Today it is known as "capacity building", and it has entered "conventional wisdom" as to what is to be done not only in Africa but throughout the developing world." – Gerry Helleiner, "The Legacies of Julius Nyerere: An Economist's Reflections," University of Toronto, Canada, 2000; also reprinted in Godfrey Mwakikagile, *Tanzania under Mwalimu Nyerere: Reflections on an African Statesman*, New Africa Press, 2000, pp. 198 – 201).

Those are just a few examples of Western leaders who had great respect for Nyerere as a leader of global stature, although he had fundamental differences with the West on a number of issues affecting the wellbeing of Africa. In fact, Western leaders were opposed to his economic policies and made a concerted effort to sabotage them. They had ideological differences with Nyerere and feared if his socialist policies succeeded in transforming Tanzania into a prosperous socialist country, capitalism, which is the bedrock of Western societies would be seriously challenged and even undermined in Africa.

They also differed with him because of his uncompromising support for the liberation struggle in the countries of southern Africa under white minority rule which were considered by Western leaders and by the white minority rulers themselves to be an integral part of the West and the custodians of Western values and civilisation in a backward and primitive continent which could also become fertile ground for communist penetration by the Soviets and the Chinese if the West did not take measures to neutralise that. But there was no communist threat. Western leaders used that in attempt to perpetuate Western domination of the continent.

Nyerere working with peasants

Although Nyerere was virtually unchallenged as a leader at home, he was from abroad, by someone who had been close to him since the fifties when the struggle for Tanganyika's independence was launched under the banner of the Tanganyika African National Union (TANU). That person was Oscar Kambona who was the secretary-general of TANU during the struggle for independence and even after the country emerged from colonial rule.

Kambona also served as minister of defence and external affairs and was the second most influential leader in the country after Nyerere. He fell out with Nyerere and left Tanzania in July 1967. He went to live in exile in Britain where he made an attempt to overthrow Nyerere by mobilising support from a number of people in Tanzania to carry out the coup. The coup was to take place in October 1969 but was discovered by Tanzania's intelligence service and was neutralised.

Years after both leaders died, there were those who tried to rehabilitate Kambona. But they did not tell the whole truth. They did not want to admit that Kambona tried to overthrow the government in spite of the overwhelming evidence that was presented in court against the coup plotters. For example, during the treason trial, Senior State Attorney Nathaniel King asked one of the coup plotters, John Lifa Chipaka, to explain what he meant when he said they were going to "eliminate the president." He wanted Chipaka to tell the court exactly what he meant when he used the word "eliminate."

Chipaka did not deny that. He did not say he did not use the expression"eliminate the president". Instead, he tried to explain by stating that they did not want to kill the president. He admitted they wanted to eliminate him but – "Eliminate him politically not physically." Those were his exact words.

Evidence was presented in court by the prosecution and by the intelligence service showing that the coup plotters also wanted to assassinate the president in addition to overthrowing the government. Kambona even became a major subject of discussion on the Internet on Tanzania's popular Jamiiforums.

One of Oscar Kambona's younger brothers, Mattiya Kambona, who years later also sought exile in Britain after Oscar did, tried to rehabilitate his brother but in an extravagant way. He even made a hyperbolic statement which impeached his credibility when he unequivocally stated: "Our elder brother Oscar, who had been Vice-President (of Tanzania)...."

It was hard to believe he made such a statement knowing full well that his brother, Oscar Kambona, had never been vice president of Tanzania.

When was Oscar Kambona vice president of Tanzania? Is it true that his younger brother Mattiya Kambona did not know that Rashidi Kawawa was vice president? Tanzania had two vice presidents. Abeid Karume who was the president of Zanzibar also served as the first vice president of the United Republic of Tanzania. And Kawawa was the second vice president, based on Tanzania mainland which is where Kambona supposedly served as "vice president," according to his brother Mattiya.

Such an outlandish claim by Mattiya was inextricably linked with delusions of grandeur the Kambona brothers were afflicted with, in their quest for power, probably even deluding themselves into believing that Oscar was indeed destined to be president of Tanzania right from the beginning.

Mattiya also brazenly stated:

"In the Tanzania that I had left, all those years ago, one scarcely saw anyone smiling: there was little to smile about in those days."

That was a downright lie.

Uninhibited, he further stated that groups of people – apparently critics of Nyerere – were routinely rounded up and thrown into prison, individuals mysteriously disappeared, and so forth. He said he expected to see that in Tanzanian newspapers when he returned home but saw none of that.

What groups of people were being routinely rounded up in the sixties and seventies? You are talking about groups of people, not just individuals. And can you name a few individuals whom Nyerere killed for criticising him? In his article reprinted below in its entirety, Mattiya Kambona apparently uses the term "disappeared" in another context as well, as a euphemism for "murder," not just for imprisonment.

And nowhere did he mention that his elder brother Oscar was the ring leader of a treasonous coterie whose inner circle included some of Kambona's close relatives; nor does he concede that the plot to overthrow the government and assassinate Nyerere started before July 1967 when Oscar Kambona left Tanzania.

One of Kambona's close associates, Eli Anangisye, was arrested in the same year. His arrest had nothing to do with criticising the government in Parliament. Of all members of parliament, it would have been Modest Chogga who would have been arrested for criticising the government relentlessly. There was even a time when Kawawa asked Chogga – "Is there not one good thing the government has done?" – since Chogga was such a persistent critic of the government.

Mattiya should also be glad that Nyerere left Oscar Kambona alone when Oscar returned to Tanzania. Here is someone who wanted to assassinate Nyerere. Here is someone who also continued to lie about Nyerere – claiming that Nyerere stole a lot money during his presidency, among other things. He also lied about Kawawa and another cabinet member Amir Habib Jamal. He said both stole a lot of money. He promised to tell it all in his speech at Jangwani Grounds in Dar es Salaam. He never did. There was nothing to tell.

In spite of all that, Mwalimu Nyerere did not retaliate against him.

It was also Mwalimu who forgave Bibi Titi Mohammed, Eli Anangisye and others who wanted to overthrow and eliminate him. How many African leaders have forgiven those who wanted to overthrow and assassinate them?

Eli Anangisye was not taken to court. That is why details about his involvement in the plot to overthrow Nyerere were not provided to the public. But he asked for forgiveness and Mwalimu forgave him and even let him get a very good job after he was released from detention. He was given a job at NATEX (National Textiles) where he was in charge of the office he worked in. I even remember where his office was. It was located near the Askari Monument in the commercial centre of Dar es Salaam. Mattiya Kambona should have known the generosity Nyerere extended to Anangisye, given the close ties Anangisye had with Oscar Kambona.

This is what Mattiya Kambona wrote in *The Salisbury Review*:

Exile and Return

Editorial note: *The Salisbury Review has had a long connection with the Kambona family and three brothers have now written for it. Oscar Kambona was a prominent Government Minister in the sixties but resigned in 1967 in protest at the introduction of the one party state and the brutal collectivization of the countryside. He left Tanzania for a 25 year exile in Britain and terrible reprisals were taken against his family and friends. (v SR vol 3 No 4, Vol 9 No 4, Vol 12 No 2, Vol 23 No 2, Vol 26 No 4)*

When President Julius Nyerere's dictatorship of Tanzania finally came to an end in 1998, my close relatives gradually became more at ease when they spoke to me on the telephone. I had been living in exile in Britain for more than thirty years, and during that time conversations with people 'back home' had necessarily been very guarded. Then one day I was somewhat surprised when someone asked me, 'When are you coming home?'

During the dictatorship I had spent more than ten years in prison (without ever having been accused of any crime) so I could not understand why my people seemed so keen for me to return to a place which could be so dangerous. Had my relatives become Government agents? Cautiously I contacted some friends who assured me that it would be safe for me to return. 'Come back', said one, 'the dark days are gone. So I decided to visit my country to 'test the waters'.

In 1968 my brother Otini and I had had to consider escaping from Tanzania, as we had realised that our situations were precarious. Our elder brother Oscar, who had been Vice-President, had already had to flee with his wife and family because he had had a disagreement with Nyerere over establishing Tanzania as a one party state and collectivising the peasants soviet style. (see *The Time I Met Mao*, SR Summer 1990)

Oscar was bitterly opposed to any such move. One day he had a warning from a friend who was a high ranking official in the police that he would be arrested very soon for opposing the President's wishes. Nevertheless Otini and I had hoped for the best and put our trust in the International community who we hoped would protect us, or at least would speak out for us, if we were arrested, and make the world aware of our situation as they did in Nelson Mandela's case.

The British government which had so painstakingly drawn up our constitution, which provided for a multiparty state, should be concerned. Otini was working as a journalist and I was employed in the Ministry of Industry and Power. I am a Cambridge graduate so we thought perhaps we were safe.

However late at night when I was working at home, I become aware of a tremendous commotion in the street outside. There seemed to be police cars everywhere. Then came the dreaded knock on the door. The police searched my home for several hours, then told me to accompany them to Ukanga (Ukonga) prison. I thought that, perhaps, was some mistake as I was not being accused of any crime, but it was to be more than ten years before I saw the outside world again.

On that dreadful night, I realized that my brother Otini had also been arrested, although I was not able to talk to him; indeed during the following years when Tanzania was developing into a completely inefficient state where nothing worked, my brother and I, while being shunted around various prisons from time to time, were very efficiently kept apart for the whole of our incarceration. Otini was married to a girl from Martinique and had two small children, my wife was from the Gambia and I had a three-month-old daughter. Both families were immediately expelled and our properties were expropriated. It was to be ten years before we saw anything of them again.

In 1978, we were just as suddenly and inexplicably released – probably through the intervention of Prime Minister Muldoon of New Zealand, who by a fortunate chance had heard of our plight and had made it known to Nyerere that aid from New Zealand would cease unless we were released. This happened almost immediately.

We were still not safe, however, as it was common practice that when people were released from prison the President would order their re-arrest. We knew that we would never be given official permission to leave the country; we would have to escape.

One day we went north to Moshi, a town near the border with Kenya. We were not sure where we would go from there, but by another lucky chance, I met a man whom I had known in Moshi prison. He agreed to take us to a path in the forest from where we could cross to Kenya. Under no circumstances, however, could he be seen with us, because as soon as the authorities realised that we were no longer in Tanzania, he would be arrested and put into prison again, as it would be assumed that he had helped us escape. We could only make our way after dark and he would have to return before dawn. And so we managed to reach Kenya.

Here we had friends. President Kenyatta, who knew Oscar, was no admirer of Julius Nyerere. We were able to travel with the help of these friends to London and safety, or so we thought. We applied to the Callaghan government for asylum, which was refused. Then one morning I received a letter from the Home Office signed personally by Dr David Owen, who was Home Secretary, to go to Heathrow Airport, for deportation back to Tanzania.

I was in a complete panic: some day I should like to confront Dr Owen and ask him why he was so keen to send us back to certain death.

Fortunately, thanks to the delay pending an appeal there was a change of government at the 1979 election and Margaret Thatcher's government granted me asylum. I was safe and free at last.

And now thirty years later after working for the Sickle Cell organization and later with Alliance Security and having retired, I decided to return to Tanzania to ‘test the waters'. On the plane from Heathrow to Nairobi I was very happy – I was back in Africa but afterwards my heart began to sink. Had I made a terrible mistake? Had my desire to see my country blinded me to the dangers that I could be facing? As the plane approached Dar-es-Salaam I began to feel that I could be experiencing my last moments of freedom. Would there be government agents waiting at the airport? After all, I had not had permission to leave the country. Perhaps I was stupid to have returned.

As the plane flew over the city I saw Ukanga (Ukonga) prison where I had spent so many months and I felt on the point of collapse. 'Dear God, help me', I prayed almost aloud. I tried to take comfort from a favourite saying of my brother Otini – 'God is greater than human beings' but all I could think about was those government agents who would undoubtedly be waiting to take me to Ukanga probably after taking me first to an interrogation room within the airport building.

As I put my foot on Tanzanian soil for the first time in thirty years I was extremely nervous and shaking almost uncontrollably. I felt that I was jumping from a comfortable warm bath into a boiling cauldron. As we entered the airport building I felt that my years of freedom were coming to an end.

I looked around me, but did not recognise any of the officials. I chose to give my documents to a young man who looked about thirty years old - he could have been born when I left the country. In spite of his youth I was expecting that he would call someone to search my belongings after which I would be told to accompany someone to the Land Rover, which I felt just had to be waiting outside to take me to Ukanga.

I was so preoccupied with these thoughts that I scarcely heard the Immigration official tell me to go on my way. I thought that I had misheard. Was he really waving me away?

'You mean I can go?,' I heard myself asking.

'Yes of course,' came the rather startled reply, 'What else do you want'?

I could keep my freedom. I surveyed the area again. I could not see a single member of Nyerere's agents around. It was amazing. My legs became light and the heavy lump sitting in my chest began to disappear.

When I left the building I thought for a moment that I must be back in London. I was surrounded by smiling faces! (In the Tanzania that I had left, all those years ago, one scarcely saw anyone smiling: there was little to smile about in those days) As we drove away I kept looking behind. Nobody was following us. Was this really my country? Yet I still could not help feeling that this was some kind of calm before a storm.

Next morning I gingerly looked outside into the street.

Apparently there was no informer watching the house. I began to feel that the disappearance of the all-pervasive fear, which I remembered so vividly, had infused my country with sweet fresh air. But as the saying goes 'old habits die hard'. I was not yet totally convinced and I was still worrying at every unfamiliar face.

I went into the city centre and bought every available newspaper expecting to see the names of people who had been dismissed from their jobs, which groups had been rounded up and thrown (without trial) into prison, which Trade Union officials were being harassed, which government critic or politician had been arrested or had mysteriously disappeared and had his property confiscated, but as I searched I found nothing.

I looked at the faces of the people around me, and gradually realised that of Dar-es-Salaam's four million people, only one – me – was worried about Presidential tyranny. I bought a cold drink and sat in the garden opposite the Cathedral and imagined that I could see the smiling faces of Angels. Eventually a mood of thanksgiving came over me and I thanked God for the wonderful changes that He had brought about in the wonderful country of Tanzania.

When Julius Nyerere was in power, anyone who criticised him or his government could look forward to perhaps a week of liberty. In the new Tanzania people are free to say what they like and can live and die a natural death. It was wonderful to be home!

Mattiya Kambona worked for the Sickle Cell Association and Alliance Security.
Source: Mattiya Kambona, "Exile and Return," The Salisbury Review, Autumn 2010, pp. 4 – 5.
www.salisburyreview.co.uk

The socialist era and one-party rule under Nyerere ended when he stepped down from the presidency in

November 1985. It had mixed results, successes and failures. Even some of Nyerere's critics who disagreed with his policies conceded that he did achieve a lot for his people, especially in providing social services such as free education and health care. They include fellow Africans who were critical of his socialist policies and one-party rule. One of them was Professor Ali Mazrui, a Kenyan, who knew Nyerere well for more than 30 years. He was one of the people who talked to Nyerere not long before he died.

Mazrui said the last time he saw Nyerere was at a breakfast he had with him in Pennsylvania, USA. He said he gave Nyerere a copy of a lecture he delivered at the University of Guyana and asked him what he thought about it. The lecture was on comparative leadership of three distinguished individuals, one of them being Nyerere himself.

He paid high tribute to a leader whom he had criticised through the years. Yet he also praised him all those years for being a superb intellectual, an ardent Pan-Africanist and a selflless leader who was deeply committed to the wellbeing of his people. As he stated in "Nyerere and I":

"When he was President of the United Republic of Tanzania, Julius Kambarage Nyerere's vision was bigger than his victories; his perception was deeper than his performance. In global terms, he was one of the giants of the 20th Century. Like all giants, he had both great insights and great blind spots. While his vision did outpace his victories, and his profundity outweigh his performance, he did bestride this narrow world like an African colossus.

It is also one of the ironies of my life that Julius Nyerere and I first met neither in his country (Tanzania) nor in mine (Kenya). I first met Mwalimu Nyerere at what was then Makerere University College in Uganda. That was more than 30 years ago. He had done his homework before coming to the campus. I was at the time regarded as one of the rising stars of East Africa's academia. As soon as Nyerere and I were introduced in English, he switched into Kiswahili and said 'Tunasikia sifa tu!' ['We have only been hearing of your praise!']. He made my day!

Long before I became a professor at Makerere, Nyerere had himself been a student there. He later went to the University of Edinburgh for his master's degree. Makerere and Edinburgh prepared him for the title of Mwalimu (meaning 'teacher') which he was to carry for the rest of his life. Young Julius entered the gates of Edinburgh University in October 1949.

Being both British-educated and having both been greatly influenced by Makerere were not the only bonds which Julius Nyerere and I had. After our first encounter on the Makerere campus, a complicated relationship developed.

As personalities, what did Julius Nyerere and I have in common? He was a politician who was sometimes a scholar. I was a scholar who was sometimes a politician. Indeed, President Obote once asked me in exasperation whether I knew the difference between being a political scientist and being a politician. Some of my public pronouncements in Uganda during Obote's first administration amounted to direct participation in the politics of Uganda. Nyerere shared some of Obote's exasperation with my political intrusion into matters of public policy.

Nyerere was particularly irritated when I published an article in the *Journal of Commonwealth Studies* in London accusing him of having unintentionally destroyed prospects for an East African Federation by his policies of socialism and economic nationalism. My article was titled "Tanzania versus East Africa: A Case of Unwitting Federal Sabotage." He conveyed his displeasure through the Principal of the University College of Dar es Salaam, Professor Pratt.

Nyerere and I had other areas of shared concern. He

translated into Kiswahili two of Shakespeare's plays – *Julius Caesar* and the *Merchant of Venice*. He was making available to Africa the genius of another civilisation. It was in the same period that I published an article titled "Edmund Burke and Reflections on the Revolution in the Congo." Burke, the Anglo-Irish philosopher of the 18th Century (1729-1797) had never written on the Congo. What I had done in 1963 was to apply his ideas about the French Revolution of 1789 to the revolution in the Congo in 1960. In my own way, this was the equivalent of translating Shakespeare into Kiswahili.

In another scholarly article, I also 'Africanised' the French philosopher, Jean-Jacques Rousseau (1712-1778) by applying his ideas to African affairs. Nyerere and I were trying to build bridges between Africa and great minds of Western civilisation. While Nyerere 'Swahilised' Shakespeare, I Africanised Burke and Rousseau.

With his concept of Ujamaa, Nyerere also attempted to build bridges between indigenous African thought and modern political ideas. Ujamaa, which means "familyhood", was turned by Nyerere into a foundation for African Socialism. Ujamaa became the organising principle of the entire economic experiment in Tanzania from the Arusha Declaration of 1967 to the mid-1980s.

His relations with the Kenyan political elite deteriorated further and further. He found Attorney-General Charles Njonjo particularly distasteful and arrogant as a person and reckless in his attitudes towards Kenya's neighbours. Nyerere was fond of Mzee Kenyatta, but he thought Njonjo exercised disproportionate influence on the old man. Nyerere was not sure whether to be amused or outraged when Njonjo turned any discussion on Kenyatta's mortality into something close to a capital offence!

Nyerere was against turning rulers into gods – 'Like the old Pharaohs of ancient Egypt.' Making Kenyatta immortal was like turning him into a god.

Nyerere and I remembered the proposal which was made in 1964 to celebrate annually the day of Kenyatta's arrest by the British as 'the Last Supper.' There was such a strong negative reaction from Christian churches in Kenya against using the concept of "the Last Supper" in this way that the idea was dropped.

My own strongest disagreements with Nyerere concerned Zanzibar and Nigeria. Did Tanganyika unite with Zanzibar to form Tanzania under pressure from President Lyndon Johnson of the United States and Prime Minister Sir Alec Douglas Home of Britain who did not want Zanzibar to become another communist Cuba? Nyerere bristled when it was suggested that the union with Zanzibar was part of the Cold War and not a case of Pan-Africanism.

Nyerere's recognition of Biafra in the middle of the Nigerian civil war was another hot subject. I personally did not share the suspicion that Nyerere recognised Biafra because the Igbo were fellow Roman Catholics claiming to be threatened by Muslim Northerners in Nigeria. But I did believe in one Nigeria and therefore disagreed with Nyerere's policies. Nyerere also bristled if it was suggested that he was ungrateful to Nigeria which had helped him with his own army in1964, and wanted to create a new force.

Nyerere's involvement with Uganda was more direct. In 1971, did Julius Nyerere convince Milton Obote to leave Uganda and go to Singapore to attend the Commonwealth conference of Heads of State and government? Milton Obote had hesitated about going to Singapore because of the uncertain situation in Uganda. Did Nyerere tilt the balance and convince Obote that he was needed in Singapore to fight Prime Minister Edward Heath's policy towards apartheid South Africa? Obote's decision to go to Singapore was disastrous for himself and for Uganda. In Obote's absence, Idi Amin staged a military coup and overthrew Obote. Eight years of tyranny and terror in Uganda had begun.

I never succeeded in getting either Nyerere or Obote to confirm that it was Nyerere who convinced Obote to leave for Singapore. But we do know that Nyerere was so upset by the coup that he gave Obote unconditional and comfortable asylum in Tanzania. Nyerere also refused to talk to Idi Amin even if the policy practically destroyed the East African Authority which was supposed to oversee the East African Community. Was Nyerere feeling guilty for having made it easy for Amin to stage a coup by diverting Obote to Singapore?

I shall always remember Nyerere's speech in Tanzania upon his return from Singapore. I was in Kampala listening to him on the radio. Nyerere turned a simple question in Kiswahili into a passionate denunciation of Idi Amin. Nyerere's repeated question was 'Serikali ni kitu gani?' ('What is government?'). This simple question of Political Science became the refrain of denouncing usurpation of power through a military coup. It was a powerful speech to his own people and against the new 'pretenders' in Kampala.

I visited Milton Obote at his home in Dar es Salaam during his first exile. Obote and I discussed Idi Amin much more often than we discussed Julius Nyerere.

One of the major ironies of my life is that I was introduced to my own founder president of Kenya, Mzee Kenyatta, by President Obote before Amin's coup.

We were all at a major ceremony of the University of East Africa in Nairobi in the 1960s. I knew Obote far better than I knew Kenyatta. Obote took me to Kenyatta to introduce me!

In 1979, Nyerere paid his debt to Milton Obote. His army marched all the way to Kampala and overthrew the regime of Idi Amin. My former Makerere boss, Prof Yusufu Lule, succeeded Idi Amin as President of Uganda. But Nyerere was so keen on seeing Obote back in power that Nyerere helped to oust Lule. Was Nyerere trying to negate the guilt of having encouraged Obote to go to Singapore for the Commonwealth Conference way back in 1971? Was that why Nyerere was so keen to see Obote back in the presidential saddle of Uganda in the1980s?

Unfortunately, Obote's second administration was catastrophic for Uganda. He lost control of his own army, and thousands of people perished under tyranny and war. Was Julius Nyerere partly to blame?

'The two top Swahili-speaking intellectuals of the second half of the 20th Century are Julius Nyerere and Ali Mazrui.' That is how I was introduced to an Africanist audience in 1986 when I was on a lecture-tour of the United States to promote my television series: The Africans: A Triple Heritage (BBC-PBS.) I regarded the tribute as one of the best compliments I had ever been paid. In reality, Mwalimu Nyerere was much more eloquent as a Swahili orator than I although Kiswahili was my mother tongue and not his.

In the month of Nyerere's death (October 1999), the comparison between the Mwalimu and I took a sadder form. A number of organisations in South Africa had united to celebrate Africa's Human Rights Day on October 22. Long before he was admitted to hospital, they had invited him to be their high-profile banquet speaker.

When Nyerere was incapacitated with illness, and seemed to be terminally ill, the South Africans turned to Ali Mazrui as his replacement. I was again flattered to have been regarded as Nyerere's replacement. However, the notice was too short, and I was not able to accept the South African invitation.

It is one of the ironies of my life that I have known the early Presidents of Uganda and Tanzania far better than I have known the Presidents of Kenya. Over the years, Julius Nyerere and I met many times. Milton Obote was one of the formative influences of my early life, in spite of our tumultuous relationship.

Ngugi wa Thiong'o (the novelist) and I were marginalised by the Kenyatta regime in spite of the fact that Ngugi and I wanted to become Kenyatta's literary biographers. When Daniel arap Moi was still Vice-President, I was considered a possible speech-writer for him in order to strengthen his credentials for the Presidency. I never played that role. Since he became President, the Moi regime and I have had an ambivalent relationship. I have never been formally introduced to him as President.

With Julius Nyerere and I, it was a bond of genuine ups and downs. Nyerere was once angry with me because I had written a citation for an honorary doctorate which was too long. The honorary doctorate was for an elderly American academic, and Nyerere was awarding the degree as Chancellor of the University of East Africa (which at that time consisted of the campuses of Makerere, Nairobi and Dar es Salaam).

As University Orator, I had written the citation, and was reading it as the elderly gentleman knelt before Nyerere. My oration was indeed too long. Nyerere did not speak to me that evening after the ceremony. He deliberately snubbed me. He had been disturbed that the elderly recipient of the honorary degree had to kneel for so long while I delivered the oration praising him. I had not struck the right balance. I felt truly chastised by the Mwalimu.

Let me also refer to Walter Rodney. He was a Guyanese scholar who taught at the University of Dar es Salaam and became one of the most eloquent voices of the left on the campus in Tanzania. When Walter Rodney returned to Guyana, he was assassinated.

Chedi Jagan, on being elected President of Guyana, created a special chair in honour of Walter Rodney. Eventually I was offered the chair and became its first incumbent. My inaugural lecture was on the following topic: "Comparative Leadership: Walter Rodney, Julius K.

Nyerere and Martin Luther King Jr."

After delivering the lecture, I subsequently met Nyerere one evening in Pennsylvania, USA. I gave him my Walter Rodney lecture. He read it overnight and commented on it the next morning at breakfast. He promised to send me a proper critique of my Rodney lecture on his return to Dar es Salaam. He never lived long enough to send me the critique.

Nyerere's policies of Ujamaa amounted to a case of Heroic Failure. They were heroic because Tanzania was one of the few African countries which attempted to find its own route to development instead of borrowing the ideologies of the West. But it was a failure because the economic experiment did not deliver the goods of development.

On the other hand, Nyerere's policies of nation-building amount to a case of Unsung Heroism. With wise and strong leadership, and with brilliant policies of cultural integration, he took one of the poorest countries in the world and made it a proud leader in African affairs and an active member of the global community.

Julius Nyerere was my Mwalimu too. It was a privilege to learn so much from so great a man." – (Ali A. Mazrui, "Nyerere and I," in *Voices*, Africa Resource Center, October 1999: Professor Ali Mazrui writes a memorial tribute on the special bonds between him and the late Mwalimu Julius Nyerere, one of Africa's few great statesmen.)

Mazrui became a highly respected and influential scholar in the sixties when he went to teach at Makerere University College in Kampala, Uganda. His first book was *Towards a Pax Africana: A Study of Ideology and Ambition*, published in 1967, developed from his doctoral thesis at Oxford.

He stated in some of of his writings and interviews years later that his dissertation was inspired by Nkrumah's

46

political thought; especially Nkrumah's pan-African daring in his quest for immediate continental unification under one government and the establishment of an African High Command to liberate the rest of the countries still under white minority rule (Nkrumah even contemplated sending Ghanaian troops to Rhodesia to topple Smith), defend the continent, and maintain peace without external assistance and interference in African affairs by world powers. Hence Pax Africana, a concept reminiscent of Pax Romana, Pax Britannica, Pax Americana, and even Pax Sovietica. As Mazrui himself stated years later about the profound influence Nkrumah had on him:

"The African leader who influenced me most positively was Kwame Nkrumah of Ghana, although I met him face-to-face only a couple of times. I had far less personal contact with him than I have had with at least a dozen other African leaders. So in what sense was Nkrumah such an influence on me? The impact was intellectual and political rather than personal. My doctoral thesis at Oxford University was partly influenced by his ideas on Pan Africanism (See my first book ever *Towards a Pax Africana: A Study of Ideology and Ambition*).

Kwame Nkrumah also stimulated my vision of Africa as a convergence of three civilizations — Africanity, Islam and Western culture. Nkrumah called that convergence 'Consciencism.' I later called it 'Africa's Triple Heritage.' I was able to elaborate on my own concept in a BBC/PBS television series titled *The Africans: A Triple Heritage* (1986)." – (Ali A. Mazrui in IGCS Reporters, "Ali A. Mazrui, Witness to History?," Special Edition Newsletter, Institute of Global Cultural Studies (IGCS), Binghamton University – State University of New York, Vol. 7, Issue 1, Spring 2008, p. 2).

His dissertation at Oxford, "The Idea of Self-Government and the Idiom of Nationalism in Some

Commonwealth African Countries, 1957 - 1963," was later published as *Towards a Pax Africana: A Study of Ideology and Ambition* after he earned his doctorate in 1966. Earlier, Mazrui had also shown leadership qualities when his fellow African students at Manchester University in England – where he obtained his bachelor's degree – elected him president of the African students union.

Mazrui would have become a UN employee after graduating from Oxford had it not been for the intervention of Colin Leys, a British scholar who was a professor of political science at Makerere during that period – it was he who also fast-tracked Mazrui's career to professorship at Makerere because of the confidence he had in the young man's academic potential. He was vindicated by history as Mazrui swiftly rose to prominence in the academic arena on a global scale. It was he who convinced Mazrui to go to Makerere instead of pursuing a career as an international civil servant at the United Nations. Leys also once taught at Kivukoni College in Dar es Salaam. As Mazrui himself stated:

"When I was a graduate student at Nuffield College, Oxford, in the 1960s, and was agonizing about my future career, the ultimate choice was between becoming an international civil servant at the Secretariat of the United Nations in New York, on the one hand, and pursuing a full-time academic career, on the other. There then walked into my life Colin Leys, a British academic who was then the professor of Political Science at Makerere in Uganda, and had once been a Don at Oxford. Colin Leys had heard about me, and came to Oxford in 1962 explicitly to persuade me to join him at Makerere.

One of the arguments which persuaded me to abandon the idea of serving at the Secretariat of the United Nations was Colin Leys' proposition that an academic career would enable me to serve the United Nations in other ways from time to time. I agreed to join Leys at Makerere

– one of the most important decisions of my life, and one which I have never regretted." – (Ali A. Mazrui, "Fifty Years as a Part-time Westerner: A Self-Portrait," *Annual Mazrui Newsletter No. 29*, Early 2005, p. 5).

Mazrui was also known for popularising the concept of Pax Africana in academic circles and even among some members of the African political elite more than any other scholar.

Credit goes to Nyerere for being the first leader to enforce Pax Africana, peace enforced and maintained by Africans themselves, on their own initiative, and on their own terms; not by forces – even if they are African – mobilised under UN auspices or that of any other non-African organisation.

Among all African countries, it is Tanzania which has given concrete expression to the concept of Pax Africana, sending troops, on its own, on pacification campaigns in Uganda, Mozambique, the Seychelles, Comoros, the Democratic Republic of Congo, and would probably have done so in Rwanda to stop the genocide had Nyerere been in power during that period.

It was Nyerere who started that. No other African leader had done that before. Nkrumah would have been the first to enforce Pax Africana had he succeeded in sending Ghanaian troops to Rhodesia to remove the white minority regime from power but was ousted before he could launch his mission (which would have needed the support of Tanzania and Zambia). So, instead of Nkrumah, it was Nyerere who came to put Pax Africana into practice years later.

As far back as 1961, Nyerere supported formation of an African High Command to pacify Congo (then Congo-Leopoldville), defend Africa and impose peace on countries which degenerate into chaos. As he stated in a speech to the Second Pan-African Seminar, World Assembly of Youth (WAY), in Dar es Salaam in August

1961:

"During the difficulties in the Congo, when the idea of an African High Command was first proposed, I was very taken with it. I do think we in Africa should think seriously of a method by which that idea could be put into practice....It provides a real force for the defense of Africa against external aggression."– (Julius K. Nyerere, excerpts from a speech delivered to the Second Pan-African Seminar, World Assembly of Youth. Reprinted from *WAY Forum*, No. 40, September 1961, in Paul E. Sigmund, Jr., ed., *The Ideologies of the Developing Nations*, New York: Frederick A. Praeger, Inc., 1963, p. 210).

Professor Mazrui also stated that there was not a single African leader who was a strong supporter of the liberation movements like Nyerere:

"Nyerere was second to none in that commitment....He became the toughest spokesman against the British on the Rhodesian question. His country played a crucial role at the OAU Ministerial meeting at which it was decided to issue that fatal ultimatum to Britain's Prime Minister, Harold Wilson – 'Break Ian Smith or Africa will break with you.'" – (Ali A. Mazrui, "Nkrumahism and The Triple Heritage: Out of The Shadows," Third Lecture, Aggrey-Fraser-Guggisberg Memorial Lectures, University of Ghana, Legon, 2002).

Tanzania became the first country to sever diplomatic ties with Britain, followed by Ghana and Egypt the next day.

Nyerere's commitment to African liberation was also underscored by Professor Piero Gleijeses in his book, *Conflicting Missions: Havana, Washington, and Africa, 1959 - 1976*:

"Of all the African leaders who proclaimed their support for the liberation struggle in Africa - Nkrumah, Nasser, Ben Bella, Sekou Toure - he (Nyerere) was the most committed. And by the second half of 1964, spurred by events in Zaire and the obvious failure of peaceful attempts to end white rule in southern Africa, this commitment, and his disappointment with the Western powers, was increasingly evident.

By the time Che arrived (in 1965), Dar es Salaam had become the Mecca of African liberation movements....Dar es Salaam 'has become a haven for exiles from the rest of Africa,' the CIA lamented in September 1964. 'It is full of frustrated revolutionaries, plotting the overthrow of African governments, both black and white'....

In September 1964, Frelimo, the movement against Portuguese rule in Mozambique, had launched the opening salvo of its guerrilla war from bases in southern Tanzania, its only rear guard.

Following Stanleyville, Nyerere had thrown his full support to the Simbas, and Tanzania had become their main rear guard and the major conduit of Soviet and Chinese weapons for them.

It was also the seat of the Liberation Committee of the OAU. The head offices of Frelimo and a host of other movements struggling against the white regimes in South Africa, Namibia, and Rhodesia were in Dar es Salaam.

The Cuban embassy there was, the CIA reported accurately in March 1965, 'the largest Cuban diplomatic station in sub-Saharan Africa.' The ambassador, Captain Pablo Ribalta, was a close friend of Che Guevara." – (Piero Gleijeses, *Conflicting Missions: Havana, Washington, and Africa, 1959 – 1976*, Chapel Hill, North Carolina, USA: The University of North Carolina Press, 2002, pp. 84 and 85).

Trevor Grundy, a British journalist who worked at the *Standard*, renamed *Daily News*, in Dar es Salaam in the late sixties and early seventies, wrote the following about Nyerere (a graduate of the University of Edinburgh) in his review of *Nyerere: The Early Years*, a book written by Thomas Molony, a senior lecturer in African studies at the University of Edinburgh, in spite of the fact that he disagreed with Nyerere's socialist policies:

"I worked in Dar es Salaam (1968-1972) for one of the English papers he nationalized in 1970....

He got into Edinburgh and that city and the people he met there left an indelible mark on his future career. Julius fell in love with the British and their great writers, economists and philosophers.

He went on to use his Edinburgh years to great advantage, bewildering (some might say bamboozling) liberal-minded journalists in the 1960s and 1970s with his formidable intellect which was the result of his reading of Jacques Rousseau and John Stuart Mill, T.H. Green's *Principles of Political Organization*, Benard Bosanquet's *Philosophical Essay of the State* and Harold Laski, the famous London School of Economics theorist.

He had a blotting paper brain.

Hardly a soul at Edinburgh guessed he would turn into Africa's number one brain box in years to come. As the historian George Shepperson put it in a BBC interview: 'We at Edinburgh were very surprised in the mid-1950s when Dr Nyerere's name became widespread throughout the world press. We never felt when he was here that he was going to become a leading politician.'

Statesmen and journalists were amazed at his knowledge....

With his eager tongue, (and) a formidable intellect,...he is presented by Commonwealth groupies as the politician who did the most to mastermind the downfall of Portuguese and British/Afrikaner rule in Africa....The Rhodesian leader Ian Smith several times referred to Nyerere as Africa's 'evil genius.'"

Professor Mazrui also wrote highly influential articles about Nyerere in *Transition*, a scholarly journal published in Kampala, Uganda, in the sixties. It was founded by a Ugandan, Rajat Neogy, who was also its editor. It was a highly intellectual publication. Its articles by Mazrui and other scholars focusing on Nyerere and Tanzania were highly analytical and intellectually stimulating, as were the rest on other subjects, and provided an insight into one of Africa's most influential leaders.

A devout Muslim and prominent Islamic scholar, Professor Mazrui also defended Nyerere, a Catholic, when some people said Nyerere recognised Biafra because the secessionists, who were mostly Igbo, were fellow Catholics; and that he authorised military intervention in Uganda to defend Christians against a Muslim dictator, Idi Amin. As he stated in his lecture at Cornell University in October 1999 in which he paid tribute to Nyerere:

"Has Nyerere's political behaviour sometimes reflected his upbringing as a Catholic? One school of thought explains his recognition of the secessionist Biafra as a form of solidarity with fellow Catholics against a Federal Nigeria, which would have been dominated by Muslims. This was in the middle of the Nigerian civil war. The Igbo of Biafra were overwhelmingly Roman Catholic.

I personally did not share the suspicion that Nyerere recognized Biafra because the Igbo were fellow Roman Catholics claiming to be threatened by Muslim Northerners in Nigeria....It seems much more likely that Nyerere recognized Biafra for humanitarian reasons.

Less convincing is the assertion that Nyerere's military intervention in Uganda in 1979 was motivated by a sectarian calculation to defend a mainly Christian Uganda from the Muslim dictator Idi Amin. In reality, Nyerere might once again have been more motivated by a wider sense of humanitarianism and universal ethics. He was also defending Tanzania from Idi Amin's territorial appetites." – ("Africa's Mwalimu: Ali Mazrui Pays Tribute to Julius Nyerere," in *Worldview Magazine*, Washington, D.C., Vol. 12, No.4, Fall 1999; also Ali A. Mazrui, "Mwalimu's Rise to Power," in *Daily Nation*, Nairobi, Kenya, 17 October 1999).

Mazrui was a bona fide scholar not a religious bigot.

When he was a young scholar teaching at Makerere – he was in his early thirties – Mazrui differed with Nyerere on a number of issues, especially during the sixties, but later conceded that he came to admire him even more through the years and agreed with him on a number of fundamental issues, unlike in the past when he strongly disagreed with him although even then, back in the sixties, he was a great admirer of Nyerere as a superb intellectual and an ardent Pan-Africanist.

In his book *On Heroes and Uhuru-Worship: Essays on Independent Africa*, Professor Mazrui described Nyerere as "the most original thinker" among all the leaders in Anglophone Africa; Senghor in Francophone Africa. And there are those who say Nyerere was "Africa's most original thinker" among all the leaders in the post-colonial era. When Nyerere died, Mazrui had the following to say about Mwalimu:

"In global terms, he was one of the giants of the 20th century.... He did bestride this narrow world like an African colossus....Julius Nyerere was my Mwalimu too. It was a privilege to learn so much from so great a man." – (Ali A. Mazrui, "Nyerere and I," ibid.)

Not long before Mazrui himself died (what a tragic loss), he said in an interview:

"I knew Nyerere very well."

54

They also met many times. Therefore, his assessment of Nyerere as a leader and as an intellectual comes from someone who personally knew Mwalimu for more than 30 years.

Professor Mazrui also said he had great respect and admiration for Nyerere as an intellectual; he towered over most of the leaders in the world. That was a very high compliment from someone who was also a critic of Nyerere. As Mazrui stated about 10 years after Nyerere died:

"Intellectually, I admired Julius K. Nyerere of Tanzania higher than most politicians *anywhere in the world* (emphasis added)." – (Ali A. Mazrui, in "Witness to History: Interview with Ali A. Mazrui," in *The Gambia Echo*, Banjul, Gambia, 25 July 2008).

Jonathan Power, a British conservative who once worked in Tanganyika and who was highly critical of Nyerere's policies and one party-rule, also paid high tribute to Nyerere in spite of the ideological differences he had with him. As he stated in his article, "Lament for Independent Africa's Greatest Leader":

"His extraordinary intelligence, verbal and literary originality... and apparent commitment to non-violence made him not just an icon in his own country but of a large part of the activist sixties' generation in the white world who, not all persuaded of the heroic virtues of Fidel Castro and Che Guevara, desperately looked for a more sympathetic role model.

Measured against most of his peers, Jomo Kenyatta of Kenya, Kwame Nkrumah of Ghana, Ahmed Sekou Toure of Guinea, he towered above them. On the intellectual plane only the rather remote president of Senegal, the great poet and author of Negritude, Leopold Senghor, came close to him." – (Jonathan Power, TFF Jonathan

Power Columns, "Lament for Independent Africa's Greatest Leader," London, 6 October 1999).

Professor Haroub Othman, a Tanzanian, also delivered a lecture at the University of Cape Town focusing on Nyerere's intellect and achievements. The title of the lecture was "Mwalimu Julius Nyerere: An Intellectual in Power." It was the first Mwalimu Nyerere Memorial Lecture and was delivered on 14 October 2005:

"I want first of all to thank the East African Students Society, and the University of Cape Town in general, for organising this occasion to commemorate the death of Mwalimu Julius Nyerere; and for inviting me to give this lecture on someone I very much respect and admire.

In my life I have met many African leaders, and if I could mention a few, and in order not to cause offence, only dead ones: Kwame Nkrumah of Ghana, Ahmed Sekou Toure of Guinea, Ferhat Abbas of Algeria, Augustinho Neto of Angola, Samora Machel of Mozambique, Amilcar Cabral of Guinea Bissau and Cape Verde, and Oginga Odinga of Kenya.

I have also met several South African leaders, including historic personalities such as Oliver Tambo, Yusuf Dadoo, Walter Sisulu, Govan Mbeki, Alfred Nzo, Duma Nokwe and Joe Slovo.

But Mwalimu Nyerere was not just a leader; he was a statesman. I have deliberately avoided calling him a politician, because politicians come and go. Statesmen live on – the impact of their presence in society is felt for many years after their death. If I can paraphrase William Shakespeare, the good they do lives after them. I found Mwalimu Nyerere to be most articulate, supremely good at putting complex issues in very simple language and very effective in relating to his audience.

Many definitions have been rendered as to who is an intellectual. Is it somebody who has been to a university

56

or, as Ali Mazrui once put it, 'one who is excited by ideas and has acquired the ability to handle some of these ideas effectively'?

Is it a professional or one who can stand up and talk on Picasso, Leo Tolstoy or Beethoven?

Byron considered an intellectual not only a person attracted to ideas, but whose purpose in life, whose thought and actions were determined by those ideas.

Issa Shivji holds that one of the important attributes of an intellectual is 'the ability to laugh at ourselves.'

I consider an intellectual as not only a person who is able to analyse the present but is also able to articulate ideas that would have a lasting impact on those who receive them.

But whatever definition one might adopt, of importance is the fact that the role of an intellectual in any society is enormous.

Western education in Africa, especially in Southern Africa, is a recent phenomenon. Pre-colonial African societies, with few exceptions, had no formal educational systems. But if the purpose of any education, as Julius Nyerere put it, 'is to transmit from one generation to the next the accumulated wisdom and knowledge of the society, and to prepare the young people for their future membership of the society and their active participation in its maintenance and development,' then these societies had appropriate educational systems.

The aim of Western education, which came with colonialism, was to instil in the minds of its recipients an idolisation for the superiority of the colonial master. First it was the sons of chiefs and other traditional leaders that received this education; and later, with the expansion of the colonial economy, more and more people acquired it. Budo, Kisubi, Fort Hare, Makerere, were all created for that purpose. The aim was to produce clerks, teachers, priests, agricultural extension workers, hospital assistants, and others, to help in the running of the colonial machinery.

University education was restricted to only a few. It was only after independence that education became accessible to more people. Of the few that received western education, not all acted according to the expectations of the colonial regime. Some turned out to be the most vehement opponents of the colonial system not only in the political and economic spheres, but also in the areas of education, culture, and others. The reasons are obvious.

Colonialism affected both the traditional chief and the ordinary worker. It did not even allow the emergence of the native capitalist. While in the colonial possessions of Asia and semi-colonial China, a local compradorial class was allowed to exist, in most of Africa this class did not emerge. It is no wonder then that in most of the African states the harbingers of the nationalist movements were people coming from the colonial bureaucracy.

The countries of Southern Africa are not a homogeneous group. There are differences in history, culture and experiences. Even those that were ruled by the same colonial power, like Zimbabwe and Tanzania, or Angola and Mozambique, have differences in their social compositions and levels of economic development. There are amongst them countries that attained independence peacefully, such as Tanzania and Swaziland, and others, like Mozambique, Angola and Zimbabwe, which attained it through the barrel of a gun.

Due to the specific conditions of the countries of the region, each one traversed the independence path in her own way. And each country brought to the fore of the independence movements a group of individuals who by any definition can be called intellectuals. What was common in almost all the countries is the fact that this group comprised people with the highest commitment to the ideals of independence and dedication to their achievement.

The backgrounds of this highly politically active intelligentsia vary. In the case of Tanzania Mainland whose economy was basically peasant-based and where education in the early colonial days was mostly provided by Christian missionary schools, the products of such a set-up were people whose vision did not go beyond the peasant collective. This was different from a place such as South Africa where a large section of the community had been uprooted from their land, a numerically strong working class had been formed and where an independent political organisation of this class existed. The logical tendency in this kind of situation would be to produce intellectuals who, to quote Amilcar Cabral, would know where the struggle for national independence ends and the struggle for social emancipation begins.

One of the successes of the colonial system in the region was that it was able to produce an academia that was dependent on Western intellectual production. This intelligentsia understood what was taking place in other societies, but lacked adequate knowledge of its own societies. This is what prevailed for a very long time in the African universities.

Admittedly, a few individuals were to be found in the universities who went against the general mould, but the pattern was for the universities to be replicas of their Western peers. As Mwalimu Nyerere stated, 'Our universities have aimed at understanding Western society, and being understood by Western society, apparently assuming that by this means they were preparing their students to be – and themselves being – of service to African society.' The University of Dar es Salaam was the first in the region to break out of this mould.

Started in 1961 as a constituent college of the University of East Africa (itself enjoying a cooperative status with the University of London), the University College of Dar es Salaam became a full university in 1970 when a decision was taken by the three East African states to each form its own national university. The University of Dar es Salaam in its curricula and research agenda tried to break away from the paradigms set up by others. It aimed at inculcating a sense of commitment to society, and tried to make all who came into contact with it accept the new values appropriate to the post-colonial society. There was a deliberate attempt to fight intellectual arrogance because it was felt that such arrogance had no place in a society of equal citizens.

The University of Dar es Salaam also played its part in the intellectual development of the region. In the ten-year period from 1967 to 1977, the university was a major cooking pot of ideas, and provided a splendid platform for debate and discussion. No African scholar, leader or freedom fighter could ignore its environs. While the government brought its official guests to see its picturesque, Mount Olympus-like exterior, others came to seek knowledge or refine their ideological positions. Here, the East and West Germans, who officially were not talking to each other; the Chinese and the Americans, who officially could not stand each other; and the white and black South Africans, who at home could not even sit together in the same church, met in the seminar rooms built by Swedes and the British to debate not only on Tanzania's development path but also the Vietnam war, the Palestinian Question, apartheid, the Chinese Cultural Revolution and countless other subjects. Very intense were these debates, and a huge number of discourses and manuscripts were churned out.

That kind of atmosphere existed partly due to conditions created by the Arusha Declaration – the country's policy document on Socialism and Self-Reliance – and partly due to the liberal-mindedness of Mwalimu Julius Nyerere who was the university college's Visitor, and after the establishment of the University of Dar es Salaam, its first Chancellor. But one also must not underestimate the impact that the presence of the liberation movements had on Tanzania's intellectual development. These movements were not only engaged in struggles in their respective countries, but their leading cadres, as a result of these struggles, were forced to constantly refine their theories and assumptions; and they found the university campus an excellent testing ground for that exercise.

Thus during the course of this process, the liberation movements not only brought in their towering figures, but also their dissidents and the harbingers of future conflicts. From FRELIMO of Mozambique came people like the religio-tribalist Rev Urio Simango, the liberal-minded nationalist Dr Eduardo Mondlane, and the Marxist poet Marcelino dos Santos; from the ANC of South Africa, people like Duma Nokwe, Joe Jele and Ambrose Makiwane; PAC brought Lebalo and Gora Ebrahim; and the MPLA of Angola, Agostinho Neto and the future Nito Alves elements. The Communist Party of South Africa brought in its towering giants, Yusuf Daddoo, Moses Mabhida and Joe Slovo.

Since I am in Cape Town, I should also mention that the Unity Movement also had its people appearing on the Dar es Salaam campus. Some of the most significant statements of these movements were made at the University Hill, including the famous one by Neto in 1974, before Angola's independence, on 'Who is the Enemy?' that has remained to this day the MPLA's weightiest document.

Sometime the staff houses on campus were turned into seminar rooms or places for social interaction. There were even times when they were used as hideouts when some leaders of liberation movements did not want their presence in the country publicly known. I remember occasions when Yusuf Dadoo and Joe Slovo (and if my memory does not fail me, Thabo Mbeki, the present President of South Africa, too) came to the university to 'reflect.'

The Tanzanian press at the time provided a very useful platform for debate and discussion. *The Nationalist* (the ruling party's paper) was under the editorship of Benjamin Mkapa, the current President of Tanzania; and the government newspaper, *The Standard*, was under the headship of Dr Frene Ginwala (the former Speaker of the South African Parliament}, as Managing Editor and Mwalimu Nyerere was the Editor-in-Chief. Apart from providing the news, these newspapers also published articles of high quality, and opened their pages for serious debates both on internal and international issues.

People from different parts of the world came to teach at Dar es Salaam. They were brought by different reasons. There were some who simply needed an African experience, but in a surrounding appeasing to their consciences; there were others who were moved by the country's revolutionary potential, and being internationalists, felt that they needed to contribute; and still others, taking pauses from their own struggles, needed breathing space and periods of reflection.

It was definitely the most international university one could ever find in the Third World.

Some of the people who came were directly from schools themselves and therefore Dar es Salaam constituted their 'baptism'; others were accomplished academics with international renown. Names of South Africans that easily come to mind are those of Ruth First, Archie Mafeje, Dennis Brutus, Willy Kogkositle (the former husband of the present Speaker of the South African Parliament), Harold Wolpe, Bob Leshoai, Sixghashe, Dan O'Meara and his former wife, Linzi Manicom and Tshabalala (the former husband of the present South Africa Minister for Health).

From within the Eastern and Southern Africa region, there came Nathan Shamuyarira who later on became Foreign Minister of Zimbabwe; Ibbo Mandaza, Miti and Frank Mbengo, all also from Zimbabwe; Orton Chirwa, the first Justice Minister in Malawi, and his wife, Vera (now a member of the African Commission for Human and People's Rights) and Mutharika, the brother of the present Malawian President; Tunguru Huaraka from Namibia; Mahmoud Mamdani (who is known to this university), Yash Tandon and Dan Nabudere from Uganda; and Yash Ghai from Kenya.

But people came also from far flung areas, including Guyanese historian and political activist Walter Rodney; the Hungarian economist Tamás Szentes; the Nigerian political scientists Okidigbo Nnoli and Claude Ake; the Ghanaians Aki Sawyer and Emanuel Hansen; the British historians Terence Ranger and John Illiffe, political scientist Lionel Cliffe and economists John Loxley and Peter Lawrence; the Canadians, Cranford Pratt who in fact was the first Principal of the university college and John Saul; and many others from Denmark, the United States and other shores.

When I was in the then German Democratic Republic in 1985 for a conference on African studies, I found out that many of their Africa specialists had been to Dar es Salaam.

Many people, like Boutros Ghali, who was a university professor before he became a Minister in Egypt and later on the first African Secretary-General of the U.N., and Adebayo Adedeji, the former Executive Secretary of the U.N. Economic Commission for Africa, included a stopover at the University Hill in their schedule whenever they happened to be in Dar es Salaam.

Yoweri Museveni, a few months before he marched into Kampala, went to the university campus to see his old friends; and on his first state visit to Tanzania, he went to deliver a public lecture at the university.

The Rivonia heroes, after their release from Robben Island prison, passed through Dar es Salaam on their way to Sweden to meet Oliver Tambo, and they came to the university to talk to the community.

Many academics have achieved fame from intellectual works they produced while in Dar es Salaam. Walter Rodney's legendary book, *How Europe Underdeveloped Africa*, that of Clive Thomas, *On Problems of Transition*, and Tamás Szentes' classic, *The Political Economy of Underdevelopment*, were all written in Dar es Salaam.

The university was not only a haven for radical scholars and activists; the students also found it an exciting and productive experience.

Issa Shivji, in his student days, had already produced *Tanzania: The Silent Class Struggle*; and the current President of Uganda, Yoweri Museveni, Kapote Mwakasungura who later on became Malawian High Commissioner to Zimbabwe, Salim Msoma, the present Principal Secretary in the Tanzania Ministry of Transport and Communications, and Andrew Shija who after graduation joined the Tanzania Army, left their classrooms and joined FRELIMO cadres in the liberated areas of Portuguese-ruled Mozambique.

A Canadian political scientist, John Saul, when teaching at Dar es Salaam University, did the same thing. The students' journal, *Cheche* [The Spark], subsequently *Maji Maji*, was very much sought after, and the teaching staff vied with each other to have their articles published in it.

From its inception in 1961 as a university college until 1985 when he stepped down as the Chancellor, Mwalimu Nyerere played an important role in the shaping of the university, and took a keen personal interest in its intellectual development. I do not think there was any national institution that he visited as many times as the university.

Mwalimu Nyerere was born on 13th April 1922 in the small village of Butiama among a minority ethnic group in Tanzania. He grew up in typical African village surroundings, and later on in life became the embodiment of the African struggle for freedom and national

64

independence and a symbol of people's aspirations for social emancipation and human fulfilment.

It was at the age of 12 that he started going to school, and only after coming of age was he confirmed to Christianity. From Tabora School, the citadel of African education at the time in the then Tanganyika, he then proceeded to Makerere College in Uganda to acquire a Diploma in Education. Makerere was at that time the highest institution of learning in East Africa, and constituted an important period for Mwalimu Nyerere in formulating the objectives and principles that guided him later on in his life. After he left Makerere, he stated the following:

'While I was at Makerere I understood that my Government was spending annually something in the neighbourhood of 80 pounds on my behalf. But that did not mean very much to me: after all, 80 pounds is only a minute fraction of the total amount which is collected every year from the African tax-payers. But today that 80 pounds has grown to mean a very great deal to me. It is not only a precious gift but a debt that I can never repay.

I wonder whether it has ever occurred to many of us that while that 80 pounds was being spent on me (or for that matter on any of the past or present students of Makerere) some village dispensary was not being built in my village or some other village. People may actually have died through lack of medicine merely because eighty pounds which could have been spent on a fine village dispensary was spent on me, a mere individual, instead. Because of my presence at the college, (and I did nothing to deserve Makerere) many Aggreys and Booker Washingtons remained illiterate for lack of a school to which they could go because the money which could have gone towards building a school was spent on Nyerere, a rather foolish and irresponsible student at Makerere.

My presence at the college therefore deprived the

community of the services of all those who might have been trained at those schools, and who might have become Aggreys or Booker Washingtons.

How can I repay this debt to the community? ...... The community spends all that money upon us because it wants us as lifting levers, and as such we must remain below and bear the whole weight of the masses to be lifted, and we must facilitate that task of lifting.'

From Makerere, Mwalimu Nyerere taught briefly before he proceeded to do a Master's degree in History at the University of Edinburgh in Scotland. He was the first Tanganyika African to acquire an overseas degree. It was in Edinburgh that his political ideas were crystallised.

Upon his return to the then Tanganyika he taught for some time in the Christian Mission schools before he threw himself fully into the nationalist struggle for independence. The Tanganyika African Association (TAA), founded in 1929 by traders and civil servants in urban areas, was basically a social organisation. Only in 1954 was it transformed into a political one, and was known as a Tanganyika African National Union (TANU); and Nyerere became its President.

As I have stated, Julius Nyerere has dominated the Tanzanian political and intellectual scene for almost five decades, and even now with his death, his influence is still felt. I will try here to briefly look at some of his ideas.

In his *Ujamaa – The Basis of African Socialism*, Mwalimu Nyerere dismissed the idea that classes had existed in pre-colonial African societies, claiming instead that these societies were living in tranquillity and peace and had experienced no antagonistic contradictions. He felt that it was possible for Africans, regardless of their social backgrounds, to come together in national movements and to retain that unity after independence. He not only dismissed the notion of the existence of classes prior to colonisation but did not see their evolution during

66

the colonial period.

In 1967 Tanzania declared its intention to build socialism on the basis of self-reliance. Julius Nyerere was definitely the intellectual power behind the Declaration. In fact Jeanette Hartmann has stated that it was written by Nyerere himself, claiming that she had seen the draft in Mwalimu Nyerere's handwriting.

The Declaration attracted huge attention. To social democrats in Europe this heralded the possibility of seeing the realisation of their ideals in an African set-up. Imperialist powers, on the other hand, were afraid that Tanzania would set up an example to the rest of Africa. From 1967, then, Tanzania's actions on the domestic and international arenas were judged in accordance with the terms of the *Arusha Declaration.*

Its close relationship with China or its acceptance of aid from the then socialist countries of Eastern Europe was seen as tendencies to further integrate Tanzania within the socialist orbit. But, as Julius Nyerere kept reiterating, the *Arusha Declaration* should have been viewed as a statement of intent. Neither in 1967 nor in 1985 when he stepped down from the Presidency was Tanzania a socialist state.

The Declaration was not without flaws and its implementation had been far from successful. There were reasons for this; but as a blueprint for development, it was something unique in Africa at that time. It was assertive and provided great hopes for millions of Tanzanians. In another paper – *Socialism: The Rational Choice* – Mwalimu argued that for a country like Tanzania, socialism was the only choice, but even if it wanted to build capitalism, that option was closed to it.

What Mwalimu Nyerere succeeded in doing was to put socialism on the national agenda. One cannot therefore agree with Ali Mazrui and many others who say that socialism was a 'heroic failure' in Tanzania. *The Wall Street Journal* declared:

67

'He fused Tanzania's 120 tribes into a cohesive state, preventing tribal conflicts plaguing so much of Africa ... Above all, he proved that it is possible to forge a nation whereby vicissitudes of ethnic affiliation are banished from social and political life. He created and promoted a powerful lingua franca, Swahili, which united and educated people.'

He preached racial and religious tolerance. Following Mwalimu Nyerere's departure from political power, the country collapsed into the arms of the IMF and the World Bank. When he left the per capita income was US$280. In 1998, thirteen years after he left, it was US$140; and school enrolment plummeted to 63%. Some of the progressive achievements of the Nyerere era are being eroded, but he will definitely be remembered in history as the person who raised the prospect of socialist development in Tanzania.

Tanzania's contribution on the question of Africa's liberation is well known. Almost all the liberation movements in Africa had enjoyed sanctuary in Tanzania. The OAU Liberation Committee had its headquarters in Dar es Salaam from the time the OAU was established in 1963. Julius Nyerere cannot be separated from the Tanzania position.

It should be remembered that as far back as 1960, when Tanganyika was not even independent, Nyerere published a pamphlet called *Barriers to Democracy* in which he castigated the white communities in Kenya, the Rhodesias and South Africa for rejecting the concept of a multiracial society based on African majority rule. Also in 1961, just before Tanganyika's independence, in an article in the London newspaper, *The Observer*, Nyerere made it clear to the British Government that the membership of independent Tanganyika in the Commonwealth will depend on South Africa either ending apartheid or withdrawing from the Commonwealth. Apartheid South Africa decided to withdraw from the Commonwealth.

As stated before, there is no single African liberation movement that did not enjoy the support of Tanzania. FRELIMO was founded in Tanzania; the ANC, after its ban in South Africa, opened its first External Mission in Tanzania; and MOLINACO, MPLA, ZANU, ZAPU, PAC and many others had Tanzania's full support. In the U.N. Decolonisation Committee (known as the Committee of 24), where Tanzania's then Permanent Representative to the U.N., Salim Ahmed Salim, held the Chairmanship for several years, and in the Non-Aligned Movement, Tanzania was in the forefront in mobilising support to the liberation struggles.

Tanzania's support to the liberation movements was not only manifested in the political and diplomatic arenas but also in the material and military fields. The Tanzanian population was mobilised many times to give material support to the liberation movements. The Tanzania People's Defence Forces trained thousands of military cadres of those liberation movements which wanted that kind of support. Tanzania was used as a facility for either storing or transporting different types of goods to the liberation movements.

It is a known fact that several villages along the border with Mozambique were bombed by Portuguese planes during FRELIMO's struggle for independence. All this testifies to the country's firm position on the question of African liberation. But again it was Julius Nyerere who was able not only to give an intellectual basis to this position but also to effectively articulate it.

Julius Nyerere was always non-racial in his perspective, and this at times got him into conflict with his colleagues both in the ruling Party and Government. During the days of the struggle for Tanganyika's independence, he rejected the position of the 'Africanists' within TANU who put forward the slogan 'Africa for

Africans,' meaning black Africans.

In 1958 at the TANU National Conference in Tabora when some leaders strongly opposed TANU's participation in the colonially-proposed tripartite elections, where the voter had to vote for three candidates from the lists of Africans, Asians and Europeans, Julius Nyerere stood firm in recommending acceptance of the proposals. This led to the 'Africanists' marching out of TANU and forming the African National Congress.

It is extremely worrying that this racist monster is reappearing now in Tanzania. Some politicians in their quest for power are using the racist card, as manifested both at last May's Chimwaga Congress of the ruling party, CCM, and in the on-going election campaigns. It is very unfortunate that no stern measures are being taken against this trend, thus giving the impression that the country's leadership is condoning it.

Again, after independence, when a section of the leadership of TANU and that of the trade union movement, the Tanganyika Federation of Labour, were demanding Africanisation of the civil service, Julius Nyerere was talking of Tanganyikanisation, thus giving a non-racial content to the whole idea.

His commitment to African Liberation stemmed not only from these anti-racist convictions but also from his strong belief that it is evil and wrong for a foreign power to colonise another people, and that it is equally wrong for a racial minority to oppress a racial majority. Mwalimu Nyerere had never doubted that whites in Zimbabwe or South Africa had the same rights as their black compatriots.

Julius Nyerere believed in peaceful means in the struggle to achieve certain political ends. He tried very much during the Tanganyika independence struggle to steer the independence movement along peaceful lines. Even at those times when the temperature was high and militants either in TANU or TFL were calling for confrontation, Julius Nyerere continued to call for restraint. When, after being convicted of libel in a colonial court, he was faced with the option of going to prison or paying a fine, he chose the latter, not so much because he did not want to be a political prisoner, but because it was felt that in his absence things might go wrong and violence might erupt.

From left: Kenneth Kaunda, Samora Machel, Julius Nyerere

However, when faced with a situation where all peaceful means were closed, Mwalimu Nyerere never hesitated to advocate the use of violence against an oppressive regime. A few months before Britain handed over power to the Sultan's regime in Zanzibar, he appealed to the British Government, through its Colonial Secretary, to reconsider its intention because he felt that if the situation was not rectified to allow the majority to peacefully take over power, then violence was inevitable. And on this he was right, because four weeks after independence the Sultan's regime was violently overthrown by opposition parties.

Again, when nationalists in Angola, Guinea-Bissau, Mozambique, the then Southern Rhodesia and South Africa were forced to take up arms against colonial and apartheid regimes, Mwalimu Nyerere committed both Tanzanian resources and his own personal prestige in helping the liberation movements to engage in the armed struggle, and found this to be in no contradiction with his non-violence convictions.

Mwalimu Nyerere's last visit to the University of Dar es Salaam was in December 1997 when he came to take part in the international conference on "Reflections on Leadership in Africa – Forty Years after Independence." The conference was in honour of his 75th birthday and was organised jointly by the Institute of Development Studies of the University of Dar es Salaam and the Mwalimu Nyerere Foundation.

Nkrumah Hall at the university, with a capacity 500 to 600 people, was full to overflowing. The organisers had expected not more than 100 people. Ministers, leaders of political parties, academics, students (even though the University was on Christmas vacation), NGO activists, foreign diplomats, media people – they were all there. It was obvious that the centre of attraction was Mwalimu Nyerere, and they all came to see him and hear him.

After the keynote address by Tanzania Vice President, the late Dr. Omar Ali Juma, Mwalimu Nyerere was asked to speak.

He spoke for more than one and half hours, entirely extempore. It was one of his best speeches, unfortunately the last one at the university. It was full of humour, but also deeply serious, thought provoking, and providing a sense of direction. The audience loved him.

The speech has been produced in full in the book that I edited based on the conference papers called *Reflections on Leadership in Africa – Forty Years after Independence*, and was published in 2000 by VUB University Press in

Brussels, Belgium.

In that speech, Mwalimu was making one very important point, that Africa South of the Sahara was on its own. North America, meaning the United States and Canada, had to do something to help Mexico, otherwise the Latin wanderers would simply cross over even if a steel wall was erected. The Slavs, Croatians, Czechs and others in Eastern Europe would be attracted to Western Europe, and North Africans would be interested in Southern Europe. The South East Asians would be looking to Japan. But Africans South of the Sahara had no 'uncle' to depend on. We were on our own. We have to rely on ourselves, and to cooperate among ourselves.

After the opening ceremony, the conference went into workshops. In the workshops where Mwalimu Nyerere was participating, he was very active, speaking with his usual lucidity of elaboration and illustration. In one session, the audience was pensive, watching him exchange views with Issa Shivji on the land question; and at another he explained why he had to ask a group of freedom fighters to leave the country, an issue that was raised in the paper presented by a Russian scholar on African affairs, Vladimir Shubin.

After one of the sessions, Mwalimu Nyerere wanted the South African academic, Patrick Bond, and a few others to follow him to his Msasani residence to continue with the discussion. Bond had raised the issue of Afrikaner capital in the Southern Africa region and the way it was behaving.

Mwalimu Nyerere's last intellectual work was the translation into Kiswahili of Plato's *The Republic*. As he was lying in bed at London's St. Thomas Hospital, he went through the manuscript, made the necessary corrections and completed them before he died. Unfortunately the work has not yet been published.

Mwalimu Nyerere was not a saint (though, according to press reports, there are discussions now amongst the

Catholics in his native area to request the Church to start the process of beatifying him) and he did commit a number of mistakes. But his patriotism was unmistaken, his commitment and devotion to Africa unquestionable and his integrity outstanding. His achievements were many, and leaders in Tanzania (and in Africa), present and future ones, will be judged according to the yardsticks set by people like Mwalimu Julius Nyerere.

At present the Southern African sub-continent is facing a deep crisis: legacies of colonialism and white domination, underdevelopment, debt problems, HIV/AIDS and natural and unnatural calamities. All these pose serious challenges to the intelligentsia of the region. The intellectuals of the colonial past could have been lured to the colonial trappings but decided to join the independence movement. The present intelligentsia have nothing to lure them into the post-colonial state. Our role is to transform our societies and to give content to human dignity." – (Haroub Othman, "Mwalimu Julius Nyerere: An Intellectual in Power," the first Mwalimu Nyerere Memorial Lecture, delivered at the University of Cape Town, South Africa, 14 October 2005, published in *Pambazuka News*, 13.10.2009, Issue 452; also in Chambi Chachage and Annar Cassam, eds., *Africa's Liberation: The Legacy of Nyerere*, Oxford, UK: Pambazuka Press, and Kampala, Uganda: Fountain Publishers, 2010; and in Saida Yahya-Othman, ed., *Yes, In My Lifetime: Selected Works of Haroub Othman*, Dar es Salaam, Tanzania: Mkuki na Nyota, and Dakar, Senegal: CODESRIA Publications, 2014).

Regardless of what his critics say, there is no question that Nyerere was a formidable intellectual. And nothing is going to diminish his stature as a thinker and as a world leader.

The American secretary of state, Dr. Henry Kissinger, an arrogant intellectual and a formidable opponent who was hated by many of his colleagues at the State

Department because of his arrogance and who tried to intimidate his adversaries in the international arena, met his equal in terms of intellectual power when he came to Dar es Salaam in 1976 to talk to Nyerere about southern Africa, Rhodesia in particular, and how to end white minority rule in the region.

Nyerere with Kissinger in Dar es Salaam in 1976

William Yandell Elliott who was one of Kissinger's professors at Harvard and who also was his adviser when he was a doctoral candidate told him years later: "Henry, you're brilliant. But you're arrogant. In fact you're the most arrogant man I've ever met. Mark my words, your arrogance is going to get you in real trouble one day." – (William Yandell Elliott, in Greg Grandin, *Kissinger's Shadow: The Long Reach of America's Most Controversial Statesman*, New York: Metropolitan Books, 2015).

Kissinger's dissertation was on Napoleonic era

diplomacy.

Elliott himself was a highly influential figure. He was presidential adviser for many years and served both Democratic and Republican administrations.

Kissinger's contemptuous attitude even towards national leaders was demonstrated when he went to Jamaica in December 1975 on a private visit. But he also had something else on his mind during that visit: Cuban troops in Angola.

He was staying with his wife at a resort in the northwestern part of Jamaica and asked Prime Minister Michael Manley, a close friend of Fidel Castro, to go and see him. That was very disrespectful and extremely arrogant for Kissinger to say that and very insulting to Manley. Manley, being prime minister, refused to go there. Instead, he asked Kissinger to go down to Kingston and see him at Jamaica House, the prime minister's official residence. Kissinger did so. He wanted Manley to condemn Castro for sending troops to Angola. Manley refused to do so. Instead, he defended Castro's involvement in Angola where Cubans were fighting the South African armed forces.

Manley's uncompromising stand and refusal to condemn Cuban involvement in Angola infuriated Kissinger; Manley also got along very well with Nyerere and the two leaders shared the same position on many issues including their attitude towards the United States as an imperialist power and strong supporter of apartheid South Africa. That is why, in pointed reference to South Africa and the United States as well as other Western powers supporting the apartheid regime, Nyerere asked a rhetorical question in an interview with American journalists in the late seventies (on ABC, "Issues and Answers"):

"Why are Western countries arming South Africa? Why are you arming South Africa? Against what military combination? And you expect us to sit just like that."

At a rally in Kingston, after his meeting with Kissinger, Manley vehemently condemned apartheid South Africa and its supporters, hence the United States, and defended Cuban involvement in Angola, drawing a thunderous applause from the people at the rally. A man of great oratorical skills who was also highly articulate, Manley said among other things:

"Now there are certain people in the world who say now why are we taking this risk to anger the United States of America. And the answer is this: We are not angering the United States of America, they are angering themselves. We have friendship with Cuba as part of a world alliance of Third World nations that are fighting for justice for poor people in the world. They are not going to tell me what kind of relationship I have with Fidel Castro. And I tell you as a party leader, as long as this party is in power, we intend to walk through the world on our feet and not on our knees."

Months later, in June 1976, Nyerere articulated the same position on Cuba's involvement in Angola. When he was asked on American television, ABC, "Issues and Answers" programme, if he knew who was behind the instability in Angola, he responded:

"I believe the CIA. Who is doing it? Who else could be doing it? Why do we keep on hearing these whispers coming from Washington, saying, 'Let us create another Vietnam for the Russians in Angola'?...You are causing *us* trouble."

He was also asked:

"Can you use your influence, which is tremendous

influence, and ask Castro to withdraw his troops from Angola?"

Nyerere responded:

"Even if I had that kind of influence, it would be unnecessary. First, you remove the cause."

"Will you commit troops (in a war against South Africa)?"

"Yes, I will commit troops. We would rather hang together than hang separately."

Kissinger denied the United States was involved in Angola. He lied, typical of his arrogance, thinking he could get away with anything including insulting other leaders, and in spite of the evidence showing the United States was deeply involved in Angola.

His lies and arrogance were also based on his belief that it was necessary to "create your own reality," as he once put it, in terms of how the United States should formulate and conduct its foreign policy.

Yet, after repeatedly denying American involvement in Angola, Kissinger later conceded: If the United States allowed the Soviet Union to project its capabilities so far away in Angola, far beyond its traditional sphere of influence, that would threaten and even destabilise the whole international system.

Nyerere took a different position. He and Manley never changed their position on the involvement of Cuban troops in Angola which they felt was justified; also, the Soviet Union continued to supply weapons to the Cubans and the MPLA forces in Angola. Kissinger equally maintained his position that Cuban troops should leave Angola since they were a threat to American geopolitical interests in Africa, a continent he arrogantly wanted to be dominated by the

West or which he felt was already an integral part of the Western sphere of influence.

Kissinger's arrogance and his disrespect for Prime Minister Michael Manley still rankled many Jamaicans years later.

A destabilisation campaign by the United States that was already underway to undermine Manley, because of his socialist orientation and strong friendship with Castro, was intensified; Kissinger was well-known for his policy of destabilisation to undermine leaders and governments he considered to be "unfriendly" to the United States; one of the best examples being the socialist president of Chile, Salvador Allende, who was overthrown in September 1973 in a military coup supported by Kissinger and the CIA.

ITT, in collaboration with the CIA, played a major role in facilitating Allende's ouster; it also worked together with the CIA, the United States Agency for International Development (USAID), and the AFL-CIO to overthrow President Joao Goulart of Brazil in 1964. The coup, authorised by President Lyndon B. Johnson, was masterminded by the CIA. Other American agencies, including the United States Information Service (USIS), renamed the United States Information Agency (USIA), have been involved in nefarious schemes – engineered, facilitated, and masterminded by the CIA – to undermine, weaken and overthrow governments in Third World countries; some of the prime targets being in Africa. They also have been known to formulate their own programmes, approved by the American authorities, to undermine governments considered to be a "threat" to American interests, despite professions to the contrary.

USAID is a very good example of CIA penetration of Third World countries because of its extensive network of workers and projects. The CIA has used USAID as a very good cover for its agents for decades since the sixties. Many USAID employees are CIA agents working in Africa, Asia, Latin America, the Caribbean and other parts of the world, dispensing foreign aid, while they are also busy working as spies for the American government.

The CIA also has been highly notorious for infiltrating academia in African countries and other parts of the Third World and for recruiting foreign students to work for the agency. Kissinger himself, who was once a professor at Harvard before entering government service, was very much in favour of such penetration. He knew how foreign students could be recruited and nurtured to serve American interests especially when they returned to their home countries and became national leaders or high-ranking government officials.

One example of such infiltration of academic institutions in Africa involved a visiting American scholar, Dr. Stephen Andrew Lucas, at the University of Dar es Salaam (UDSM) in the late sixties and seventies. He taught at UDSM for seven years. He was a lecturer in sociology and was a CIA agent, seasoned and highly accomplished. He served as a CIA agent in Congo during the turbulent sixties before he came to Tanzania. He worked under Larry Devlin who was the CIA station chief in Leopoldville when Lumumba was arrested and assassinated. Devlin died at his home in Virginia, USA, on 6 December 2008. He was 86.

Dr. Lucas also worked as a CIA agent in Angola, Mozambique and Madagascar. When he retired, he was awarded "the Defense Intelligence Director's Award and Retirement Medallion and Certificate of Distinction."

He died in Italy on 24 May 2006 when he was on vacation with his wife. He was 69. He was buried in his home state of Oklahoma in the United States.

Before his death, Dr. Lucas was a professor at Louisiana State University where he was the executive director of international programmes. He also taught Swahili among other subjects.

The case of Dr. Lucas, with regard to Tanzania and other countries where CIA agents are assigned, demonstrates how the agency does everything it can to infiltrate governments to the highest levels. His obituary states, among other things:

"He taught at the University of Dar es Salaam for seven years and served as an advisor to Tanzanian President, Julius Nyerere."

That may be coded language, saying he was "an advisor" to President Nyerere. What it obviously means is that he was able to establish contacts at the highest levels of the Tanzanian government to spy for the United States probably even without the knowledge of the Tanzanian intelligence service during that period.

It also happened in Ghana where the CIA station chief in Accra, Howard T. Bane, who was the mastermind of the military coup against Nkrumah, was able to penetrate security and establish contacts at the highest levels of government in preparation for the coup. The British intelligence service, MI5, also had an agent in Accra, John Thomson, who infiltrated the Ghanaian government during that period and was equally involved in Nkrumah's ouster.

Soon after Nkrumah was overthrown, Thomson "unofficially" congratulated the head of the new military regime, General Joseph Ankrah, on behalf of the British government, for getting rid of Nkrumah. Thomson and Ankrah drank a bottle of brandy to celebrate Nkrumah's downfall. The military junta formed the National Liberation Council (NLC) to rule Ghana. Nkrumah dismissed it as the Notorious Liars Council. It was fully controlled by the United States. As Christopher Andrew states in his book, *Defend The Realm: The Authorized History of MI5*:

"Thomson went on to be welcomed by, and deliver unofficial congratulations to, the NLC chairman, General Ankrah, and the other NLC members. On 2 March, following a favourable report from Thomson, Britain formally recognized the new Ghanaian regime, establishing full diplomatic relations three days later. This was the only occasion on which a Security Service officer was charged by HMG with making the first contact with a new government which had seized power in a *coup d'etat*." – Christopher Andrew, *Defend The Realm: The Authorized History of MI5*, New York: Alfred A. Knopf, 2009, p. 471. See also Christopher Andrew, *For the President's Eyes Only: Secret Intelligence and the American Presidency from Washington to Bush*, New York: Harper Perennial, Haprer Collins, 1996).

Nyerere with Nkrumah in 1963

Two years before the 1966 coup, the United States was already plotting to overthrow Nkrumah. In February 1964, the CIA director told the head of foreign operations at the

State Department that Ankrah was the right person to replace Nkrumah. The American embassy in Ghana was already working with opposition groups to depose Nkrumah.

The British were also, right from the beginning together with the Americans, deeply involved in the plot to overthrow Nkrumah. A cable sent to the Home Office in London from the British High Commissioner in Accra, A.W. Snelling, bluntly stated that the British establishment had to get rid of Nkrumah because he was making the Africans too politically conscious; not just in Ghana but across the continent and beyond. He expressed his exasperation at Nkrumah's Pan-African militancy and commitment to Africa's wellbeing more than four years before Nkrumah was overthrown and did not hide his dislike for the Ghanaian leader. As Gamel Nasser Adam states:

"Britain was more forthright in its abhorrence of the rise in awareness among the African people. Earlier on the British High Commissioner in Ghana at the time, A.W. Snelling in a dispatch dated 5th September 1961 sent to the Commonwealth Relations Office in London, noted Nkrumah's '...knack of giving expression to the feelings of so many Africans, who are all the time rapidly becoming more and more politically conscious, is exasperating. I can well understand the fury he arouses in London, and often share it myself.'

In other words halting the rising tide of African consciousness of liberation was a major priority of those forces which wanted to maintain the status quo of colonial and neo-colonial consciousness." – Gamel Nasser Adam, "Constructing National Consciousness in Russian Literature: Some Lessons for the African Milieu," in Helen Lauer, Nana Aba Appiah Amfo, Jemima Asabea Anderson, eds., *Identity Meets Nationality: Voices from the Humanities*, Legon-Accra, Ghana: Sub-Saharan Publishers, 2011, p. 236).

The British saw Nkrumah as a threat to Western interests in Africa, a position shared by the United States government which stated that Nkrumah had done more than any other African leader to undermine American interests in Africa. Therefore he had to go, even if it meant assassinating him; a job the CIA is well known for, working closely with the State Department. And it continued to do so when Henry Kissinger was secretary of state, as is still the case today.

Nkrumah survived seven assassination attempts. Some of the assassination plots were supported by the CIA.

The CIA is also known for fomenting trouble in Third World countries, infiltrating the media and other institutions, state and private, to achieve its goals. Provision of funds and even weapons to groups which serve its interests is one of the tactics the CIA uses, as happened in Ghana to undermine and ultimately overthrow Nkrumah.

It also happened in Congo-Leopoldville when Lumumba was prime minister. Joseph Mobutu was already on the CIA payroll when he was Lumumba's secretary and went on to seize power with CIA support.

The CIA, which was authorised by President Dwight Eisenhower to assassinate Lumumba, even claimed the Congolese prime minister was "insane" and "a dope fiend" in an attempt to tarnish his image and discredit him as a leader. As Christopher Andrew states in his book, *For the President's Eyes Only: Secret Intelligence and the American Presidency from Washington to Bush*:

"Allen Dulles (the CIA director, also known as the DCI – Director of Central Intelligence) told Einsehower that Lumumba was insane; later reports alleged that he was also 'a dope fiend.'

On September 21 (1960) the DCI reported to an NSC (National Security Council) meeting, chaired by the president, that 'Lumumba was not yet disposed of.' Still fascinated by the use of poisons in covert action, Richard Bissell (head of CIA's covert operations) instructed a CIA scientist (Dr. Sydney Gottlieb) to prepare biological toxins designated to assassinate or incapacitate an unnamed 'African leader' (Lumumba)." – (Christopher Andrew, *For the President's Eyes Only: Secret Intelligence and the American Presidency from Washington to Bush*, New York: Harper Perennial, Harper Collins, 1997, p. 253).

The CIA also armed and funded the opposition in Jamaica when Michael Manley was prime minister. Many people were killed in clashes between Manley's supporters and members of the opposition party led by Edward Seaga who was the"darling" of the United States. Manley himself survived three assassination attempts.

In a radio interview in 1980 - at the end of his first term as prime minister - when he lost the election to Seaga whose campaign was funded and directed by the CIA, Manley said the following about Seaga: "He is a mental weakling" who was taking orders from his masters and was ready sell his country to the United States and other Western powers.

Manley's wife Beverley, an Afrocentric nationalist, in an interview years later after her husband died, recalled how she was equally offended by Kissinger when he asked her husband to go and see him at a resort in northern Jamaica:

"Kissinger was staying just outside of Ocho Rios and he asked Michael to come down there and see him and Michael talked to me about that; and I said, but I don't understand, you are prime minister, he comes to see you at Jamaica House. And then Kissinger came and saw him at Jamaica House."

One of Manley's supporters, also in an interview years later, had this to say about Kissinger:

"Kissinger doesn't come down here and stick his finger in Manley's face, you box his finger out of your face. That's almost a national call for a reaction to it. Give thanks to the fact that Manley stood up to Kissinger."

You don't go to another country and tell the leader of that country, a president or a prime minister, to come and see you at your hotel room, ordering him around, telling him what to do as if you own him and his country. You enquire first, to find out if it is even for possible for you to see him. If it is possible, then you ask for permission, and in a respectful way, to go and see him at his office or at his official residence.

But that was Henry, with his arrogance, and contemptuous attitude towards other people including national leaders, ignoring all protocol.

Had he shown any kind of arrogance when he met Nyerere, it would have been a different story. He met a strong and highly intellectual leader who was not afraid of him and whom he could not intimidate into submission. And he knew that even before he came to Dar es Salaam, what kind of leader he would be dealing with. As David Martin, a prominent British journalist who worked in Tanzania for many years – he knew Nyerere very well – and who covered southern Africa extensively, stated:

"Tanganyika became independent on 9 December 1961 and a year later when the country became a republic, Nyerere, elected by over 96 per cent of the voters, became its first president.

For the next 24 years Nyerere was to fill the African and international stage like a colossus. When he met the astute American Secretary of State Henry Kissinger for the first time in Dar es Salaam in 1976, the two men began a mental verbal fencing match of David and Goliath proportions.

One began a quote from Shakespeare (some of whose works Nyerere translated into Swahili setting them in an African context) or a Greek philosopher and the other would end the quotation. Then Nyerere quoted an American author. Kissinger laughed: Nyerere knew Kissinger had written the words.

Neither man trusted the other. Kissinger wanted the negotiations (over Rhodesia, now Zimbabwe, and southern Africa) kept secret. Nyerere, understanding the Americans' duplicity, took the opposite view and as Africa correspondent of the London Sunday newspaper, *The Observer*, I was to become the focal point of the Tanzanians' strategic leaks.That year the newspaper led the front page on an unprecedented 13 occasions on Africa. All the leaks, as Kissinger knew, came from Nyerere. One political fox had temporarily outwitted the other.

Apart from his simplicity and piercing intellect, one of Nyerere's most endearing traits was his honesty. " – (David Martin, "Mwalimu Julius Kambarage Nyerere: Obituary," Southern African Research and Documentation Centre (SARDC). A former news editor and deputy managing editor of the *Standard*, renamed *Daily News*, Dar es Salaam, Tanzania, David Martin was a founder-director of the Southern African Research and Documentation Centre (SARDC) of which Julius Nyerere was patron. He lived in Tanzania for 10 years from 1964 to 1974 and frequently talked with Nyerere through the decades, a period of 35 years, until Nyerere's last days).

Kissinger met with Nyerere three times in 1976. He met with Nyerere and Tanzania's minister of foreign affairs, Ibrahim Kaduma, 25 – 26 April. He met with Nyerere again, 14 – 15 September, when the two leaders discussed Rhodesia and Namibia. Kissinger met with Nyerere for the third time on 21 September when the

American secretary of state briefed Mwalimu on his meetings with Rhodesian Prime Minister Ian Smith and other leaders of the white minority regime in Rhodesia.

Kissinger said Nyerere was one of the toughest and most intelligent negotiators he ever dealt with. Others he named in that category included Andrei Gromyko, Soviet ambassador to the United States Anatoly Dobrynin; Chou En-Lai, and Hafez al-Assad. He said when negotiating with Gromyko, you think you are making progress, as he addresses every point you made, and then you find out he takes you right back to the beginning without making any concessions.

James Spain, who was the American ambassador to Tanzania when Kissinger came to Dar es Salaam, also recalled what Kissinger told him about Nyerere during that time:

"One of the amusing sidelights of Henry Kissinger's second or third visit was this. He stayed in the Kilimanjaro Hotel. When the party was clearing out to go to the airport, I was told that the Secretary wanted me. I went upstairs. People were carrying away files and suitcases.

In the middle of a table there was a 'bug' protector that was still making weird electronic sounds. Henry gets both of us hunched over this thing. He said 'Thank you very much. This visit has been useful. Your arrangements were fine, but I want to warn you about one thing. This fellow Nyerere is not on our side.'

This was a pretty accurate reflection of the spirit of the times." – (James Spain, quoted in an interview, *Why Tanganyika united with Zanzibar to form Tanzania*, op. cit., p. 407).

Kissinger did not get what he wanted from Nyerere. Asked at a press conference in Dar es Salaam after Kissinger's mission if he considered it to be a failure because Kissinger did not get the assurances and the concessions he wanted to get from Nyerere on how to resolve the contentious issue of white minority rule in Rhodesia and in southern Africa in general, Nyerere, quoted by David Ottaway of *The Washington Post*, responded:

'A mission of clarity is not a mission of failure.'

David Ottaway, who sent his report from Dar es Salaam, was one of the American reporters who covered Kissinger on that trip.

Kissinger got the chance to know exactly how Nyerere felt and what his stand was on the subject. He learned something from Mwalimu. As David Ottaway stated in *The Washington Post* just before Kissinger went to Africa, when Kissinger gets to Tanzania he is going to 'get a dose of African nationalism" from Nyerere. David's wife, Marina Ottaway, also covered Kissinger and Nyerere during that time. She also worked for *The Washington Post*.

Kissinger's own assessment of Nyerere reflects profound respect for Mwalimu as a leader and as a superb intellectual by someone who already had a very high opinion of himself as an intellectual and as a statesman of global stature. He did not tower over Nyerere in terms of intellect and statesmanship. As Kissinger himself stated in his book, *Henry Kissinger: Years of Renewal*, in a section entitled, "Julius Nyerere and Tanzania: The Ambivalent Intellectual":

"Tanzanian President Julius Nyerere proceeded to arrange an official reception that could not have been more cordial. The motive, however, was altogether different from Kenyatta's. Nyerere...was, at heart, deeply suspicious of American society and American intentions.

In international forums, Tanzania's ministers frequently castigated us. Nyerere would not have described

89

friendship with the United States as a national priority; instead, he tended to think of relations with us as a necessary evil....

Brilliant and charming, Nyerere had an influence in Africa out of proportion to the resources of his country, proof that power cannot be measured in physical terms alone....Because Tanzania was involved in the armed struggle that was taking place in Rhodesia, and because of Nyerere's intellectual dominance, Nyerere would be a key to any solution....

Many of Nyerere's American admirers thought he and his colleagues were the embodiment of American values and liberal traditions. By contrast, his American critics viewed Nyerere as a spokesman for Communist ideology. Neither view was accurate. Nyerere was his own man. His idiosyncratic blend of Western liberal rhetoric, socialist practice, nonaligned righteousness, and African tribalism was driven, above all, by a passionate desire to free his continent from Western categories of thought, of which Marxism happens to be one. His ideas were emphatically his own....

For our first meeting, Nyerere, a slight, wiry man, invited me to his modest private residence. It was a signal honor, and he introduced me to his mother and several members of his family. He was graceful and elegant, his eyes sparkling, his gestures fluid.

With an awesome command of the English language (he had translated *Julius Caesar* into Swahili), Nyerere could be a seductive interlocutor. But he was also capable of steely hostility. I had the opportunity to see both these sides during my three visits to Dar es Salaam....

Nyerere was the key to the front-line states....

The two most impressive leaders I encountered on this trip, Nyerere and Senghor, were at opposite ends of the African spectrum. In a sense, they represented metaphors for varying approaches to African identity.

Nyerere was a militant who used ideology as a

90

weapon; Senghor was an intellectual who had taught himself the grammar of power.

Nyerere considered himself as a leader of an Africa that should evolve in a unique way, separate from the currents in the rest of the world which Africa would use without permitting them to contaminate its essence. Senghor saw himself as a participant in an international order in which Africa and *négritude* would play a significant, but not isolated, role.

When all is said and done, Nyerere strove for the victory of black Africa while Senghor sought a reconciliation of cultures within the context of self-determination." – (Henry Kissinger, *Henry Kissinger: Years of Renewal*, New York: Touchstone, 1999, pp. 931 – 932, 936, 949 – 951).

Nyerere's high intellectual calibre, together with his humility and commitment to the wellbeing of the masses, was one of the major assets which served him well during his leadership. As Professor Mazrui stated:

"Above all, Nyerere as president was a combination of deep intellect and high integrity...(and) was in a class by himself in the combination of ethical standards and intellectual power. In the combination of high thinking and high ethics, no other East African politician was in the same league." – (Ali A. Mazrui, "Mwalimu's Rise to Power," in the *Daily Nation*, Nairobi, Kenya, October 17, 1999).

Almost four years later in September 2003 at the University of Nairobi, Professor Mazrui also had the following to say about Nyerere in his lecture, "Towards Re-Africanizing African Universities: Who Killed Intellectualism in Post-Colonial Africa?":

"The most intellectual of East Africa's Heads of State

91

at the time was Julius K. Nyerere of Tanzania – a true philosopher, president and original thinker....

Who killed intellectualism in Tanzania? In Tanzania intellectualism was slow to die. It was partially protected by the fact that the Head of State - Julius Nyerere - was himself a superb intellectual ruler. He was not only fascinated by ideas, but also stimulated by debates....Ujamaa and the justification of the one-party state stimulated a considerable amount of intellectual rationalization and conceptualization....

In my own personal life I was respected more as an intellectual by Milton Obote in Uganda and Julius Nyerere in Tanzania than I was by either Mzee Kenyatta or Daniel arap Moi.

Even Idi Amin, when he was in power in Uganda, wanted to send me to apartheid South Africa as living proof that Africans could think. Idi Amin wanted me to become Exhibit A of the Black Intellectual to convince racists in South Africa that Black people were human beings capable of rational thought." – (Ali A. Mazrui, "Towards Re-Africanizing African Universities: Who Killed Intellectualism in Post-Colonial Africa?" The lecture was dedicated to Dr. Crispin Odhiambo-Mbai of the University of Nairobi who was assassinated in Nairobi on 14 September 2003).

A staunch Pan-Africanist throughout his political career, Nyerere was resolutely opposed to imperial domination of Africa as a neocolonial entity dominated by the former colonial powers and by new ones who also wanted to dominate and exploit the continent. He was painfully aware of the phenomenon; it was prevalent in most African countries.

Years later, he recalled how the former French colonies – with the exception of Guinea under Sekou Toure and Mali under Modibo Keita – were still controlled by France; this being just one example of neocolonialism that was the very antithesis of independence. As he stated in an interview when he talked about Francophone Africa:

"I went to Addis and it was an incredible meeting (the first summit of African heads of state and government in Addis Ababa, Ethiopia, in May 1963 which led to the establishment of the Organisation of African Unity - OAU).

Here is this continent of young nations coming from colonialism and so forth and the debate is awful, and really what provoked me was the French-speaking countries, you know. With all their French culture, training in rationalization - you can't really argue with those fellows. And I discovered some of these fellows have their visas -THEIR VISAS - signed by the French ambassadors in their own countries! And I said, 'Oh, but I thought you were fighting for freedom?'" – Julius K. Nyerere, in Bill Sutherland and Matt Mayer, eds., *Guns and Gandhi in Africa: Pan African Insight on Nonviolence, Armed Struggle, and Liberation*, Africa World Press, 2000. The interview was also reproduced, from the book, by Chambi Chachage, "Excerpt from Interview with Bill Sutherland," Centre for Consciencist Studies and Analyses (CENSCA), 5 September 2008).

There were only a handful of African leaders who did their best to keep their countries independent. And they showed a remarkable degree of independence in their dealings with world powers at a great cost to their countries. One of them was Nyerere. Others were Nkrumah, Sekou Toure, Modibo Keita, Gamal Abdel Nasser, and Ahmed Ben Bella.

Nyerere was also a very close friend of Sekou Toure and Nasser. All these leaders also worked closely together. In an interview with Jorge Castaneda (the author of *Companero: The Life and Death of Che Guevara*) in Geneva, Switzerland, in 1995, Ahmed Ben Bella said there were six leaders – Nkrumah, Nyerere, Nasser, Sekou Toure, Modibo Keita, and Ben Bella himself – who formed their own secret group, known as The Group of Six, within the OAU. He said they worked together secretly on a number of issues – including the Congo crisis and the liberation struggle – vital to the wellbeing of Africa, excluding other African leaders.

The six were true African leaders, independent-minded and committed to the wellbeing of Africa.

It is a tragedy that Africa does not have leaders of that kind anymore, especially in this era of globalisation or new imperialism when the continent is being ruthlessly exploited by world powers and other outsiders, leaving Africans with nothing.

Millions of Africans have even lost their land to these outsiders. Countless have died. Millions of acres of land in many countries on the continent don't belong to Africans anymore. Tanzania's minister of foreign affairs, Bernard Membe, said in an interview with Voice of America (VOA) in 2011 that Africa has already lost hundreds of millions of acres of land the size of Germany. He added: The land does not belong to us anymore.

Leaders like Nyerere, Nkrumah and their colleagues would never have allowed that to happen.

In the case of Nyerere, his credentials as an uncompromising supporter of the liberation struggle in Africa were solidified by the contribution he and his country made for decades towards the attainment of freedom and independence in the countries of southern Africa which were still under white minority rule including the bastion, and citadel, of white supremacy on the continent: apartheid South Africa.

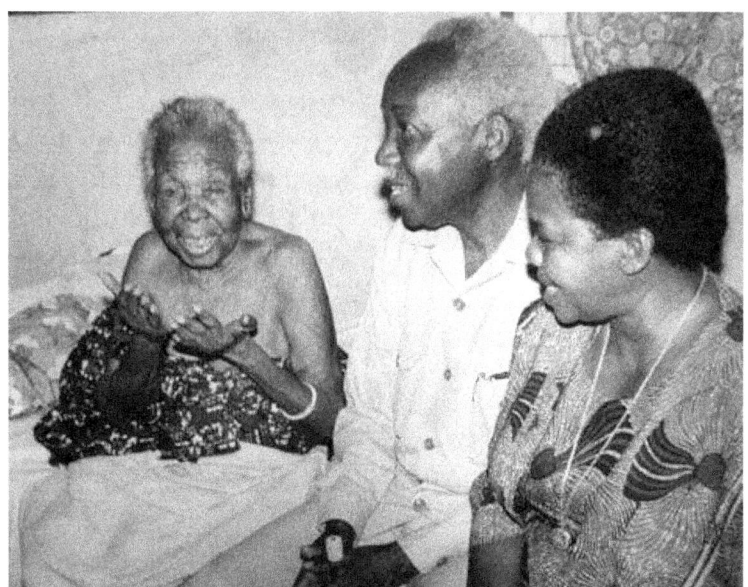

Nyerere's mother, left; Nyerere and his wife Maria, 10 November 1985, in his home village, Butiama, soon after he stepped down from the presidency.

The sacrifices Tanzania – under the leadership of Nyerere – made during the liberation struggle in southern Africa will always be remembered even if they are overlooked or ignored by some of the people we helped. One example of the contributions Tanzania made to the liberation struggle was explained by a British journalist, David Martin, after he interviewed Nyerere one day:

"I remember one day sitting in his office questioning that a number of African countries had not paid their subscriptions to the OAU Liberation Committee Special Fund for the Liberation of Africa. He looked at me for some moments, thoughtfully chewing the inside corner of his mouth in his distinctive way. Then, his decision made, he passed across a file swearing me secrecy as to its contents. It contained the amount that Tanzanians, then according to the United Nations the poorest people on earth, would directly and indirectly contribute that year to the liberation movements. I was astounded; the amount ran into millions of US dollars.

It was the practice among national leaders in those days to say that their countries did not have guerrilla bases. Now we know that Tanzania had many such bases providing training for most of the southern African guerrillas, who were then called 'terrorists' and who today are members of governments throughout the region....

Tanzania was also directly attacked from Mozambique by the Portuguese. But, in turn, each of the white minorities in southern Africa fell to black majority political rule and Nyerere saw his vision for the continent finally realized on 27 April 1994 when apartheid formally ended in South Africa with the swearing in of a new black leadership." – (David Martin, "A Candle on Kilimanjaro," in *Southern African Features*, 21 December 2001).

Then there was the enormous sacrifice the people of Tanzania made in the liberation wars in terms of lives. They lost soldiers, men and women, so that others could live and win their freedom. They did. All that was done because of Nyerere. As President Yoweri Museveni said about Nyerere:

"He was the greatest black man that ever lived. There are other black men such as Nelson Mandela and Kwame Nkrumah, but Nyerere was the greatest." – (Yoweri Museveni, quoted by *New Vision*, Kampala, 4 April 2012).

When Nyerere was on his deathbed, even some of his most bitter critics who were opposed to his economic policies paid tribute to him as a highly principled leader who did his best to help his people and Africa as a whole even if, according to them, he pursued wrong policies. But they conceded he meant well. One of them, British conservative Jonathan Power, stated the following about

Nyerere in his article, "Lament for Independent Africa's Greatest Leader":

"Tanzania in East Africa has long been one of the 25 poorest countries in the world. But there was a time when it was described, in terms of its political influence, as one of the top 25. It punched far above its weight. That formidable achievement was the work of one man, now lying close to death in a London Hospital." – (Jonathan Power, "Lament for Independent Africa's Greatest Leader," London, 6 October 1999).

Kenyan political and social analyst, who is also one of Africa's prominent columnists, Philip Ochieng, stated the following in his article, "Africa's Greatest Leader":

"Julius Nyerere is among the extremely few world leaders who have selflessly attempted great things for their national peoples....

Dar es Salaam was a Mecca of the world's national liberation movements, and a hotbed of global intellectual thought....

Mwalimu Julius Kambarage Nyerere is the most successful leader that Africa has ever produced since the European colonial regime collapsed 50 years ago....

Until his death, Nyerere, who was humble, self-effacing and selfless, continued to serve humanity on many capacities....

An intellectual of immense stature, a man of great personal integrity, a paragon of humanism, Julius Kambarage will be hard to replace in Tanzania, in Africa and on the globe. I was privileged to know and work with such a man. That is why, as I mourn, I ask, with Marcus Antonius, whence cometh such another?" – (Philip Ochieng', "Africa's Greatest Leader," *The East African*, Nairobi, 19 October 1999; P. Ochieng, "There Was Real Freedom in Mwalimu's Day," *The East African*, 20 October 1999).

It will be a long time before Tanzania gets another leader of his calibre, if at all.

Appendix I

Julius Nyerere on the Boycott of South Africa in a letter to the Editor, *Africa-South*, October-December 1959

ON JUNE 26, 1959, Julius Nyerere was the principal speaker - along with Father Trevor Huddleston - at a meeting in London, which launched the Boycott South Africa Movement. It was re-named the Anti-Apartheid Movement in 1960.

That was at a time when most African leaders were only concerned about the independence struggle and problems in their own countries. Tanganyika itself was then not yet independent. But Nyerere still felt that it was necessary for the people of Tanganyika and others to get involved in the struggle for the liberation of South Africa from apartheid. An injustice to one is an injustice to all because humanity is one. As he stated in his letter to the editor of *Africa-South*, October-December 1959:

When I was a schoolboy, a friend of mine took me to the tailor one day and had me measured for a pair of shorts. We were great friends. His was mine and mine was his. He knew I needed a pair of shorts very badly. A few days later I got my pair of shorts, well made, fitting perfectly. I was proud of myself and proud of my friend. But it was not long before I discovered how my friend had obtained the money with which he had bought that pair of shorts for me. I returned it to him immediately. I could not disapprove of the manner in which the money had been obtained and still enjoy what the money had bought for me.

It is this same principle, which makes me now support the boycotting of South African goods. We in Africa hate the policies of the South African Government. We abhor the semi-slave conditions under which our brothers and sisters in South Africa live, work and produce the goods we buy. We pass resolutions against the hideous system and keep hoping that the United Nations and the governments of the whole world will one day put pressure on the South African Government to treat its non-European peoples as human beings.

But these resolutions and prayers to the United Nations are not enough in themselves. Governments and democratic organisations grind very slowly. Individuals do not have to. The question then is what an individual can do to influence the South African Government towards a human treatment of its non-white citizens.

Can we honestly condemn a system and at the same time employ it to produce goods, which we buy, and then enjoy with a clear conscience? Surely the customers of a business do more to keep it going than its shareholders. We who buy South African goods do more to support the system than the Nationalist Government or Nationalist industrialists.

Each one of us can remove his individual prop to the South African system by refusing to buy South African goods. There are millions of people in the world who support the South African Government in this way, and who can remove their support by the boycott. I feel it is only in this way that we can give meaning to our abhorrence of the system, and give encouragement to

100

sympathetic governments of the world to act.

It is most fitting that Jamaica, that island which has solved its racial problems so well, should have taken the action it has in support of the boycott. It is equally fitting that the Trade Union Congress of Ghana should immediately have given its support. I was personally happy to participate in a meeting in London where the boycott was launched. Already the authors of apartheid are beginning to feel the sharp effect of the boycott. But they cannot feel it fully until every person in the whole world who disapproves of the South African system withdraws his support of it by withdrawing his contribution to its upkeep.

I must emphasise that the boycott is really *a withdrawing of support*, which each one of us gives to the racialists in South Africa by buying their goods. There is a very real sense in which we are part of the system we despise, because we patronise it, pay its running expenses.

We are not being called upon to make much of a sacrifice. We are not being called upon to go hungry and court imprisonment. That is the lot of our brothers and sisters inside South Africa. We are being asked to substitute other goods for South African goods, however much of a sacrifice this may mean to our suffering brethren in South Africa itself. We are not being called upon to support or not to support the oppressed in South Africa. We are being called upon to stop supporting those who oppress them.

The issue is as simple as that. Let every man and woman who disapproves of the South African system search his or her conscience, and decide to support or not to support the racialists of South Africa.

Source:

ANC Documents, African National Congress (ANC), South Africa. See also *Voices*, Africa Resource Center, On the Boycott of South Africa, by Julius Nyerere, then president of the Tanganyika African National Union (TANU), in a letter to the editor of *Africa-South*, October-December 1959.

The principle enunciated here by Nyerere, and which he upheld throughout his life, was also reflected in his conduct when he was a student at St. Mary's Secondary School, Tabora. He was appointed a prefect, overseeing other students. Because of his status, he and the other prefects were entitled to double rations. Nyerere objected to that, saying all the students were equally entitled to the same amount of food. The double rations were dropped, and there was no more double-dipping for prefects, at least not as an entitlement.

Reprinted from Godfrey Mwakikagile, *Nyerere and Africa: End of an Era*, Third Edition, New Africa Press, 2010, pp. 550 – 552.

Appendix II

Julius Nyerere of Tanzania Dies; Preached African Socialism to the World

Michael T. Kaufman
The New York Times
15 October 1999

Julius K. Nyerere, the founding father of Tanzania who used East Africa as a pulpit from which to spread his socialist philosophy worldwide, died yesterday in London. He was about 77 and was being treated for leukemia, and he suffered a major stroke last week.

An uncharacteristically humble and modest national leader whose preferred honorific was Mwalimu, the Swahili word for teacher, Mr. Nyerere led his country into independence and guided it for nearly three decades.

Idealistic, principled, and some would say naively misguided, Mr. Nyerere became one of the most prominent of the first generation of politicians to head newly independent African states as colonialism ebbed, playing a leading role in the debate over economic inequalities between the Northern and Southern Hemispheres.

When he guided what had been the British Trust Territory of Tanganyika into sovereignty in 1961, he was the youngest of the continent's triumphant nationalists, a group that included Kwame Nkrumah of Ghana, Jomo Kenyatta of Kenya, Kenneth Kaunda of Zambia and Felix Houphouet-Boigny of Ivory Coast.

When he stepped down as President 24 years later, he was only the third modern African leader to relinquish power voluntarily on a continent that by then included 50 independent states. He went neither to jail nor into exile, but to a farm in Butiama, his home village, near the shore of Lake Victoria.

Mr. Nyerere ascended to power without a single shot being fired, becoming Prime Minister and then President of a land that at the time contained nine million people affiliated with more than 120 tribes, stretching from Lake Victoria and Lake Tanganyika down to the Indian Ocean.

It was one of the poorest countries in the world. Its mostly illiterate citizens were scattered over remote regions, often unable to find a common language, although they shared ample rigors as they wrested a meager subsistence from the soil or the sea.

Early Progress, Enduring Debate

By the time Mr. Nyerere gave up the last vestiges of political power in 1990, when he retired as chairman of the single political party, Tanzania had undergone staggering, often traumatic, changes.

The population had doubled, to more than 20 million. It had merged with Zanzibar in 1964. Almost 70 percent of the people had been prodded to move from traditional lands into paternalistically planned villages -- ujamma -- in what became Africa's largest and most debated example of social engineering.

After vast investment in education, literacy rose phenomenally, and 83 percent of Tanzanians were able to read and write. Mr. Nyerere also succeeded in promoting Swahili so that it superseded dozens of tribal tongues to become a true national language.

Some Western countries, notably the Scandinavians, were so impressed that they provided billions of dollars, making Tanzania one of the 10 largest recipients of foreign aid per capita.

But it was still one of the poorest countries in the world. The year he left his party post, the World Bank reported that Tanzanians were surviving on a per-capita income of $200 a year, and that the economy had shrunk on average half a percentage point a year between 1965 and 1988.

The debate over Mr. Nyerere's leadership extended beyond his tenure, with academics, politicians and development strategists often dividing sharply over his legacy.

His domestic and international defenders, generally people of the left, praised his emphasis on social investments and his egalitarian economic policies, crediting them with creating a culturally cohesive nation that avoided ethnic conflict while life expectancy, literacy and access to water increased.

His Tanzanian supporters took pride in Mr. Nyerere's reputation as one of the most prominent proponents of a new economic order that would benefit the developing south in economic relations with the industrial north.

Mr. Nyerere also gained international prestige for his principled support of the struggles for majority rule in South Africa, Namibia, Zimbabwe, Mozambique and Angola, and for Tanzania's military counter offensive against Idi Amin of Uganda, which routed the dictator and sent him into exile. The third world honored him, and he won the respect of such Western leaders as Olof Palme, Pierre Trudeau, Willy Brandt and Jimmy Carter.

Still, his critics, who included free-market liberals and conservatives, condemned him for adopting paternalistic and coercive policies like ujamma. They deplored his insistence on one-party rule and price controls, which they said stultified Tanzania's economy, shrank agricultural production, encouraged corruption and led to vast squandering of foreign aid.

From a Modest Home To a Master's Degree

The distance Mr. Nyerere traveled from his birth to political power and to the center of an international polemic on development was enormous, spanning ages as well as years.

He was born into the Zanaki people, a small tribe of 40,000 in the hills southeast of Lake Victoria. His mother, Mugaya, was 15 years old. She had been the fifth wife of Burito Nyerere (pronounced nyuh-RARE-ee), a village headman, who was 61 years old when the boy was born. Later, as the village chief prospered, he took more wives, and when he died at 81, he had 22 wives and 26 surviving children.

Mugaya's son was named Kambarage, for a rain spirit, for it had rained on the day of his birth (though the year is uncertain, 1922 or '23). Years later, after he attended mission schools, he became a Roman Catholic and chose Julius as his baptismal name.

He lived the life of a Zanaki child, weeding his mother's garden and going off on bow-and-arrow hunts with the older men. But all that changed when the village chief, with some reluctance, agreed to send his child to board at a school at Musoma, 30 miles from his home.

Quickly, as he learned Swahili and English, he was spotted as an exceedingly bright child by the White Fathers, the priests who ran the school, and in 1936 he placed first in the entire territory on an entrance exam for a school in Tabora. At the school, which was patterned on private schools in Britain, a native elite was to be trained to help administer their homeland under British rule.

He spent six years at Tabora, in central northwestern Tanganyika, graduating in 1943. He went on to Makerere

106

University in Uganda, and after being baptized and teaching for two years in a church school, he won a scholarship to Edinburgh University, where he earned a master's degree in history and economics.

Soon after he went away to school, his father paid a lobola, or bride price, to the family of a girl from his home area as a traditional deposit on a future marriage. But at Makerere, Mr. Nyerere met a Christian girl named Maria Magige. In 1948 he asked her to marry him, and when she agreed, the six cows that his father had given to the family of the prospective child bride were returned to the Nyerere family and were passed on to Maria's parents.

Maria Magige Nyerere bore him five sons and a daughter. Mrs. Nyerere and the six children were in London when he died, Reuters reported. A state funeral is expected to be held in Dar es Salaam next week before Mr. Nyerere is buried in Butiama, his home village, in northern Tanzania.

Mrs. Nyerere was the head of the country's major women's organization, the United Women of Tanzania, and she ran a poultry business for some years while her husband was President. But she gave it up when Mr. Nyerere imposed a leadership code that forbade government officials from involvement in a private business in order to discourage corruption.

New Teacher Offers A Socialist Lesson

On his return from Scotland, Mr. Nyerere worked as a teacher in a government school. He also won election as president of the Tanganyika African Association, an elite social organization that he quickly transformed into a political party that later led the struggle for independence.

That new group, the Tanganyika African National Union, was formed on July 7, 1954, a date now celebrated as a national holiday known as Saba Saba, the seventh day of the seventh month.

When Tanganyika became independent on Dec. 9, 1961, Mr. Nyerere became its first Prime Minister, but six weeks later he suddenly resigned. He remained president of his party, Tanu, and spent nine months traveling throughout the country, meeting ordinary people and preparing a document that he issued under the title *Ujamaa: The Basis of African Socialism.*

This was the first of two defining proclamations by which Mr. Nyerere sought to blend the major influences of his life: the cooperative forces he had observed in tribal life, with their emphasis on a constant search for consensus; the ideal of a Christian brotherhood, to which he had been exposed at school, and the goals of welfare-state socialism that he had absorbed from British Labor Party teachings while he lived in an Edinburgh housing project.

In *Ujamaa* he declared:

"In acquisitive societies, wealth tends to corrupt those who possess it. It tends to breed in them a desire to live more comfortably than their fellows, to dress better and in every way to outdo them."

He then depicted traditional African society as providing sustenance to all members of a community. He wrote that in contrast to Europe, where socialism had arisen in opposition to capitalism, Africa had never known either class division or class struggle. He then concluded:

"Ujamma, or 'familyhood,' describes our socialism. It is opposed to capitalism, which seeks to build a happy society on the basis of the exploitation of man by man, and is equally opposed to doctrinaire socialism, which seeks to build its happy society on the philosophy of inevitable conflict between man and man."

Habits of Modesty And Strict Ethics

On the first anniversary of independence, Tanganyika became a republic. Portraying ujamma as the national goal, Mr. Nyerere was easily elected President.

One element of his position paper that he adopted quickly and adhered to for the rest of his public life was his disavowal of pomp and perquisites.

He never received more than $8,000 a year as President. A slight man, standing 5 foot 6 and weighing 125 pounds, he appeared both abroad and at home wearing a gray or black safari shirt over his trousers and a white crocheted skullcap of the sort worn on Zanzibar.

In contrast to many African leaders, who often raced through their capitals in motorcades with phalanxes of motorcycle outriders, he moved around Dar es Salaam in an old car with just his driver, who stopped for red lights. In his spare time he had translated *Romeo and Juliet* (he translated *Merchant of Venice*) and *Julius Caesar* into Swahili.

The second of Nyerere's proclamations was delivered in 1967 and came to be known as the Arusha Declaration, after the northern town where Mr. Nyerere read it to party leaders. It called for a commitment to self-reliance and established the leadership code, which obligated government and party officials to give up all sources of income but their salaries.

But the most important provisions established rural development as the country's chief priority.

In the following months, in town and village meetings, Mr. Nyerere expounded on this, calling upon peasant farmers to voluntarily relocate and pool their labors in collectively harvesting common fields. As he repeatedly explained, Tanzanians were too scattered for services to be brought to them. Only if they gathered in villages would they be able to benefit from schools, clinics, libraries.

Befitting the teacher he was, he often resorted to didactic slogans, which party stalwarts were quick to paint all over the country. Decades later the fading mottos can still be read on public buildings or small village shops: "Work Is the Foundation of Progress." "A Poor Country Cannot Rule Itself if It Relies on Foreign Help." "We Must Run While Others Walk."

All too often, the slogans faded in an atmosphere of lassitude.

Seven years after the Arusha Declaration, only some 1,000 ujamaa villages had been established and only 2 million of Tanzania's then 14 million people were living in them. Virtually none involved successful collective farming.

A Rocky Descent Into Economic Gloom

Mr. Nyerere displayed growing impatience, and in December 1973 he addressed his people on the radio in a scolding tone.

He said that while the Government had abolished poll taxes, ended school fees and extended water supplies and health clinics in rural areas, the people had done almost nothing in return. While the Government could not turn people into socialists by force, he said, it could insure that everybody lived in a village, and he wanted the entire country to be living in planned settlements by 1976.

What followed were campaigns of persuasion, intimidation and coercion. People were told that famine relief would be provided only to those who moved peacefully. Because transport was provided by militias and the army, party stalwarts told peasants that if they did not pull down their houses and load them on government trucks, the houses would be demolished. Many homes were burned, and there were a few cases in which people were killed.

Mr. Nyerere deplored the violence, attributing it to

110

overly zealous local officials, but he insisted that such mistakes should not obscure the success of a program that, he said, had led more than 13 million people to move into ujamaa communities by 1976, a movement of close to 70 percent of the population in three years.

The evaluations of more detached observers were far less enthusiastic. James C. Scott, a Yale agronomist, studied the Tanzanian experience for a book titled *Seeing Like a State: How Certain Schemes to Improve the Human Condition Have Failed* (Yale University, 1998).

Mr. Scott noted that in contrast to Soviet collectivization, the Tanzanian campaign was not conceived as an all-out war of appropriation. He wrote:

"The disruptions and inhumanities of Nyerere's program, however serious for its victims, were not in the same league as those inflicted by Stalin. Even so, the ujamaa campaign was coercive and occasionally violent. It proved, moreover, a failure, ecologically as well as economically."

With people moved from their traditional fields, food production plummeted. Moreover, according to outside scholars, 60 percent of the new villages were on semiarid land unsuitable for long-term cultivation.

Attempts were made to dictate the growing of certain crops, notably fire-cured tobacco, to be sold at what villagers saw as confiscatory prices set by government agencies. Peasants resisted this, and they also ignored annual work plans and production targets. With people having left their old cashew trees behind, a huge share of that once-important crop went ungathered.

Mr. Scott concluded that the failure of ujamma was virtually guaranteed "by the high modernist hubris of planners and specialists who believed that they alone knew how to organize a more satisfactory, rational and productive life for their citizens."

"It should be noted," he continued, "that they did have something to contribute to what could have been a more fruitful development of the Tanzanian countryside. But their insistence that they had a monopoly on useful knowledge and that they impose this knowledge set the stage for disaster."

Finger-Pointing Taints Search for Aid

In Dar es Salaam in the late 70's, tales of such willful and miscalculated planning were widely exchanged by the same diplomats who complimented Mr. Nyerere for his concern and decency:

* After a state agency was organized to market fish, fish disappeared from the market because fisherman no longer found it worth their while to go out.
* A Norwegian-backed training project to establish coastal shipping was not permitted to carry cargo so it would not compete with the state trucking company.
* A regulation banning doctors from treating patients privately in their homes after their work in government clinics and hospitals led to the emigration of many doctors.
* An Italian agronomist developing export crops promoted strawberries, for which there was a strong market in Europe, but a party official declared that unlike beets and potatoes, strawberries were not a socialist fruit.

Over the years Mr. Nyerere would sometimes acknowledge that Government mismanagement, particularly its abolishment of functioning producer cooperatives, had contributed to sharp declines in staple crops.

But he placed much more blame on an international economy in which agricultural prices had dropped sharply while the cost of oil, machinery and other imports had risen. He noted that for Tanzania to purchase a seven-ton truck in 1981, it had to produce four times as much cotton, or three times as much coffee, or 10 times as much tobacco as it had five years earlier.

But whatever the accuracy of those calculations, it was also true that farm production was tumbling, with sisal harvesting, for example, dropping to 33,000 tons in 1985 from 250,000 in 1964.

Desperately needing credit, Mr. Nyerere turned to the International Monetary Fund and in 1980 began a five-year struggle with the fund, resisting its dictates that he divert funds from education and emphasize export crops while allowing domestic food prices to rise. In this skirmishing, Mr. Nyerere became the third world's most assertive exponent of the new economic order in which the economic imbalance between North and South would be overcome through international law and obligation rather than through markets or charity.

But he was never able to reach an agreement with the I.M.F., and in 1984, when Tanzania could not meet interest payments to the United States, the Reagan Administration suspended all aid but emergency food allocations.

Mr. Nyerere reinforced his reputation abroad by his steadfast support of liberation movements in African countries where majority rule had not been achieved. He provided training camps for the African National Congress from South Africa and diplomatic support for national movements fighting in Mozambique and Rhodesia.

And in 1978, after Uganda annexed a 700-square-mile section of Tanzania, Mr. Nyerere angrily denounced Idi Amin, the Ugandan despot, as a man who had killed more people than either Ian Smith, the white leader of Rhodesia, or John Vorster of South Africa.

With startling bluntness, he added:

"There is this tendency in Africa to think that it does not matter if an African kills other Africans. Had Amin been white, free Africa would have passed many resolutions condemning him. Being black is becoming a certificate to kill fellow Africans."

Mr. Nyerere, who as a youthful pan-Africanist President had considered doing without an army, reasoning that such a force would be useless against great powers and therefore could only fight African neighbors, sent Tanzanian soldiers and Ugandan exile volunteers to push back Mr. Amin's forces. They routed the Ugandan dictator, who fled into exile in Saudi Arabia.

After he retired, Mr. Nyerere was often asked whether he had any regrets. In a typical interview, he said he was pleased that "Tanzanians have more sense of national identity than many other Africans," and he expressed pride in the nation's high rate of literacy. As for the poor economy, it had resulted from an "a hostile international environment," he said.

"What would I have changed if I had my time again? Not much."

The white-haired farmer, the Mwalimu, then turned to his attempts to instill his idea of African socialism.

"They keep saying you've failed," he mused. "But what is wrong with urging people to pull together? Did Christianity fail because the world isn't all Christian?"

Julius Nyerere became Tanganyika's first Prime Minister in 1961, proclaiming that Africa, unlike Europe, promised sustenance to all members of the community, an idea at the core of African socialism. He guided Tanganyika's merger with Zanzibar in 1964, forming Tanzania. In 1996 he met with President Nelson Mandela of South Africa, after he had retired to his farm in Butiama, where he is to be buried.

Dignitaries pay tribute to Nyerere

Norimitsu onishi
The New York Times
21 October 1999

Dar es Salaam, Tanzania ---Inside a stadium thronged by thousands of mourners standing and sitting under a merciless sun, leaders from all corners of Africa and officials from the West paid tribute today to Julius K. Nyerere, the founding father of Tanzania and one of the most influential independence leaders on the continent.

A line of dignitaries, including Secretary of State Madeleine K. Albright, walked along a red carpet that led into a glass mausoleum where Mr. Nyerere's body lay in an open coffin. A phalanx of military officers later draped the coffin in a flag of Tanzania, the nation born after Mr. Nyerere guided the British Trust Territory of Tanganyika to sovereignty in 1961.

Many African rulers influenced by Mr. Nyerere attended the funeral, including Robert Mugabe of Zimbabwe, Sam Nujoma of Namibia, Joaquim Chissano of Mozambique, Thabo Mbeki of South Africa and Yoweri Museveni of Uganda. Princess Anne represented Britain, and the Finnish President, Martti Ahtisaari, attended as the head of the European Union.

The streets of this seaside capital were quiet as the

Government declared a national holiday to mourn the former President, who died last Thursday in a London hospital, aged about 77. Mr. Nyerere, who had been receiving treatment for leukemia, suffered a major stroke two weeks ago.

His body was flown here to lie in state early this week. Millions of Tanzanians had filed through the stadium to pay respect to the man who ruled them from 1962 to 1985, and whom they called Mwalimu, or "teacher" in Swahili.

His support of liberation movements and his role as an elder statesman in Africa, but especially the moral rectitude for which he was equally famous, drew the praise of African leaders -- even of those from nations that do not share his socialist philosophy.

"There can be no question that Julius Nyerere was every inch a builder and one of the great leaders of our time," said Dr. Albright, who is winding down a weeklong visit through Africa.

Praise also came from ordinary Tanzanians who filled the 35,000-seat national stadium and who, for a state funeral, circulated with ease and casualness. Mr. Nyerere was remembered for building a nation out of a land with more than 120 ethnic groups, an enormous feat on a continent riven with ethnic conflicts that are often exploited by politicians.

"We've lost an important man in Africa," said Salem Mkiba, a 55-year-old civil servant, who was standing at the rear of the stadium, where the dignitaries' speeches were barely audible. "He was the real builder of this nation. Without him, I don't know where we would be. Look at our country: Tanzania is one of the only peaceful and unified countries in Africa."

But if Mr. Nyerere's funeral drew many African leaders, they also suggested how they have yet to meet Mr. Nyerere's ideal of a united Africa. Almost no president came from French-speaking African countries, as the divide with English-speaking African remains a legacy of

116

colonialism. Also, among the leaders present -- including the leaders of Eritrea, Ethiopia, Rwanda and Uganda -- many are currently at war with each other or another African nation.

President Thabo Mbeki of South Africa, his wife, Zanele, and President Olusegun Obasanjo of Nigeria, were among the African leaders yesterday at the funeral of Julius K. Nyerere.

Appendix III

Africans mourn death of the father of Tanzania

The Guardian, London, UK
15 October 1999

Julius Nyerere, former president of Tanzania and, in the two decades before the release of Nelson Mandela from prison, the most important politician in Africa, died in London yesterday aged 77, after a long battle against leukaemia. His wife, Maria, and six of his eight children had been at his bedside during the last week.

His death was mourned across Africa, where uniquely he retained his prestige both with the generation of leaders whose countries he helped in their struggles for independence and with ordinary people for whom he was the continent's one leader untainted by corruption. He was tireless in his crusade against poverty.

He will be buried at his birthplace in the impoverished remote area of Butiama. His body will be flown home after a mass at Westminster cathedral at noon on Saturday.

Tony Blair, the prime minister, said:

"He was a leading African statesman of his time and the founder of modern Tanzania. He played a historic role in consolidating independence in his country.

The fact that Tanzania is today a country at peace with itself and its neighbours is, in large part, a tribute to 'Mwalimu' Nyerere."

Peter Hain, the foreign office minister, who arrived in Dar es Salaam on a visit yesterday, said:

"Mwalimu Julius Nyerere was a grandfather to modern Africa, loved and respected by the whole continent, and the international community.

He was an inspiration to everyone involved in freedom struggles across Africa, and his passing hurts us all."

South Africa's president, Thabo Mbeki, said Nyerere was a pillar of strength for oppressed people.

His death raised the spectre of instability in Tanzania, where political in-fighting and tension over the future of Zanzibar have been rising in recent years. They had been held at bay by Nyerere's control of the ruling party - Chama Cha Mapinduzi (CCM).

His death was announced in a television and radio address by the current president, Benjamin Mkapa. He said:

"Dear Tanzanians, it is with great shock and sorrow that I announce our beloved father of the nation, Julius Kambarage Nyerere, is dead."

He added:

"I know the death of the father of the nation is going to shock and dismay all Tanzanians. Others will be filled with great doubt and fear.

Mwalimu built a foundation of unity in our country and he fought for the freedom of all. I assure all Tanzanians Mwalimu left a firm foundation."

120

State radio played funeral music while its TV station ran film of Nyerere giving speeches in parliament, meeting heads of state, and speaking with ordinary citizens.

Nyerere was the first president of Tanganyika after leading the country to independence from Britain in 1961. He masterminded union with Zanzibar in 1964, renaming his country Tanzania.

He launched an ambitious project to transform the lives of the country's 30m peasants. He was enormously successful in bringing education and health to even the remotest areas, though the collectivising of the agricultural economy largely failed and brought him ridicule from a hostile west.

In the last years before his death Nyerere was the key negotiator who stopped Burundi's ethnic violence from spilling out of control, as had happened in Rwanda in 1994, and the one voice of sanity against the unravelling of Congo.

Julius Nyerere

Julian Marshall
The Guardian, **London, UK**
15 October 1999

A giant of the African independence struggle, he retained his worldwide moral authority even after his vision of rural socialism faltered.

In his heyday as president of Tanzania - which he ruled from 1961 to 1985 - Julius Nyerere, who has died from leukaemia aged 77, was lion- ised by the liberal left of the world for his impassioned advocacy of his style of African socialism, but mauled by his critics as a priggish autocrat, whose idealism failed to deliver prosperity to his people.

To his credit, Nyerere stepped down peacefully and voluntarily, long before it became fashionable for Africa's self-appointed life presidents to subject themselves to the verdict of their peoples in multi-party elections.

In 1967 came Nyerere's Arusha Declaration, his policy on socialism and self-reliance. Its cornerstone was ujamaa, or familyhood, which was imposed on Tanzania in the following years. The aim was to collect people into villages or communes, where they would have better access to education and medical services. Nearly 10m peasants were moved and a substantial majority were forced to give up their land. But to most Tanzanians, the idea of collective farming was abhorrent. Many found themselves worse off; incentive and productivity declined, and ujamaa was effectively abandoned. It was a measure of Nyerere's international prestige that the failure of this fundamental policy at home in no way dented his global standing.

A man of austere and unostentatious personal habits, and instantly recognisable in his Mao tunic, Julius Nyerere was born at Butiama, on the eastern shore of Lake Victoria, into the small Zanaki tribe. He was 12 before he first went to school, but was immediately singled out for his lively intelligence by the Roman Catholic priests. After Makerere University, in Kampala, he taught for three years, admitting, later in life, that he was a schoolmaster by choice and a politician by accident.

In 1949 he became the first Tanzanian to study at a British university, when he went to Edinburgh on a government scholarship. And it was there, under the influence of post-war Fabian socialists, that he developed his own political ideas of grafting socialism on to African communal existence.

Nyerere left teaching in 1954, formed the Tanganyika African National Union, and campaigned for the nationalist movement. He was elected to the then Tanganyika legislature in 1958, representing East

Province, the first time that the country's Africans were enfranchised, and became leader of the opposition. He became chief minister in 1960. But it was not until 1961, when he was sworn in as prime minister of the newly-independent Tanganyika that he would be in a position to start putting the ideas into practice.

In the same year, he joined other African leaders in denouncing the racist policies of South Africa and declaring that, if the apartheid regime remained in the Commonwealth, Tanzania would never join. South Africa subsequently withdrew its membership.

For Nyerere the move marked the beginning of an effective commitment to African liberation movements: later, he played host to the African National Congress (ANC) and the Pan- African Congress (PAC) of South Africa, to Samora Machel's Frelimo - battling against the Portuguese in Mozambique - and to Robert Mugabe's fledgling Zanla forces, which opposed colonial rule in the then Southern Rhodesia. He broke off relations with Britain, Tanzania's principal aid donor, after its failure to use force when Ian Smith declared UDI in 1965 - earning himself the description by Smith of the "evil genius" behind the ensuing guerrilla war.

The unusually principled way in which Nyerere looked upon international politics was again evident in his uncompromising stand against the brutal regime of Idi Amin in Uganda in the late 1970s. Despite almost universal condemnation of the dictator's excesses, it was left to Tanzania to intervene militarily and dislodge Amin. A brief invasion of Tanzania by Amin in late 1978 brought a swift reponse from Nyerere: Tanzanian troops, joined by Ugandan exiles, were mobilised to drive back the invaders. But they didn't stop at the border. Kampala fell in 1979, with its residents lining the streets chanting the name of the Tanzanian leader. It was the first time in African post-colonial history that one country had invaded another and captured its capital. It was a fundamental breach of the principles of the Organisation of African Unity. But Nyerere weathered the storm.

However, the campaign proved expensive, and while their leader devoted such resources, time and energy to foreign affairs, his critics in Tanzania argued that he overlooked domestic problems, and failed to apply the same observance of human right abuses. He seldom flinched from using a Preventive Detention Act that allowed him to lock up his opponents virtually at will.

Relations with Zanzibar, which had united with Tanganyika in 1964 to form the United Republic of Tanzania with Nyerere as president, were always strained. Tanzania became ever more dependent upon foreign aid, and decision-making was paralysed by a ponderous bureaucracy. Nyerere was to admit that mistakes had been made, while his devotees pointed to developments - such as the spread of literacy and primary healthcare.

A practising Catholic in a predominantly Muslim country, Nyerere married Maria Magige in 1953, by whom he had five sons and two daughters. He maintained a passionate interest in Swahili, the language of East Africa, and translated *Julius Caesar* and *The Merchant Of Venice*. His political writings included *Essays On Socialism* (1969) and *Freedom And Development* (1973).

The idea that when he resigned as president, handing over to Hassan Ali Mwinyi, Nyerere would live quietly on his farm at Batiama, cultivating his interest in book-binding, was always improbable. And indeed he continued to influence government policy through his chairmanship of the single ruling party, Chama Cha Mapinduzi.

Whether or not he initiated the debate about an alternative political system in Tanzania is questionable, but he rapidly became a part of it. Although mwalimu , or teacher, as he liked to be known, was to his own people one of them, he nonetheless became - like Senghor, of Senegal, and Sadat, of Egypt - an African leader who outgrew his country.

124

When he relinquished the party chairmanship in 1990, he was able to devote more time to campaigning for greater co-operation between developing countries, and, as chairman of the South Commission, a closing of the gap between rich and poor. He also took on the role of African elder statesman, working notably in conflict resolution, although his most recent efforts – trying to resolve Burundi's civil war - did not bear fruit.

Julius Nyerere belonged to a generation of African post-independence leaders, like Ghana's Kwame Nkrumah and Zambia's Kenneth Kaunda, who had an unshakeable belief in their mission to lead their countries to a better world through their chosen political ideologies, but who were unable to recognise their personal failings.

When he stepped down, Nyerere declared that "although socialism has failed in Tanzania, I will remain a socialist because I believe socialism is the best policy for poor countries like Tanzania." His successors decided otherwise, embracing capitalism and the free market, but with arguable benefits to the country.

His detractors would regard his stewardship of Tanzania to have been flawed by his single-minded adherence to a manifestly unworkable policy. Yet Nyerere is more likely to be remembered for having provided a moral leadership to Tanzania, and indeed Africa, when the continent was taking its first shaky steps after independence.

Ahmed Rajab, editor of *Africa Analysis*, writes:

Julius Nyerere was "a great leader who made great mistakes," as one ruler once famously said of another. He unified his country, certainly, gave it a sense of purpose and, in the 1960s and 1970s, made Tanzanians feel proud of themselves.

As a pan-Africanist, he could not be faulted for putting his country in the forefront of the frontline states against white minority rule in Africa. He took a principled stand at a great cost to his country, but his people never really minded. Tanzania became a home for exiled freedom-fighters who are now the rulers in a number of southern African states.

Many a time, Nyerere confounded those of us who thought of ourselves as being to his left by appropriating our political lexicon and social agenda. He never quite became a Marxist, but the former shepherd boy, whom we used to deride as "a good boy of the west" and who was viewed with suspicion by the likes of Kwame Nkrumah, turned into a tactical ally when he started talking about class struggle and a classless society.

But his African socialist philosophy of ujamaa only brought misery and economic degradation. Under the man who preached self-reliance, Tanzania depended on foreign aid more than any other African country. That was only one of his contradictions.

His vision of a united Africa did not stop him from recognising Biafra, the breakaway eastern Nigeria, in the early 1960s. A pious Catholic, who could not tolerate the excesses of Idi Amin, Nyerere nonetheless felt himself unable to move against another dictator much closer to home: the burly Sheikh Abeid Karume, Zanzibar's then president and Tanzania's first vice-president, who presided over a brutal dictatorship, detained people without trial, killed countless imagined or real enemies, and forced girls of Persian or Arab origin to marry elderly black Zanzibaris.

Karume was assassinated in 1972 but, throughout the sheikh's eight-year rule, Nyerere never lifted a finger against his tragic histrionics.

Despite his failings, Nyerere was revered by progressive Africans. When they talked of Tanzania, they talked, in effect, of Nyerere - the simple, unassuming former schoolteacher, untainted by corruption or personal scandals and with a fondness for Mateus rosé. In the 1950s and 1960s, admirers would copy his hairstyle, his moustache, and later, when he started donning a kofia , the Swahili-Muslim cap, his fellow up-country Christians did likewise. In the mid-1960s he went to China, shook hands with Chairman Mao, and came back with a variant of the Mao suit, which became de rigueur among Tanzania's officials and aspiring politicians.

Had he not been a politician, Nyerere might have become a scholar of repute. He was a poet of modest pretensions and, although his translation of Julius Caesar was not brilliant, he did, after all, dare to translate Shakespeare. He could be profound and esoteric to the intellectuals; streetwise to the masses. His speeches were electrifying.

I remember spending the best part of two hours with him alone in a Nairobi hotel room in 1994, when he was out of office and Tanzania was about to embark on its first multi-party elections. Initially, he refused to discuss the prospective presidential candidates of his own party, the Chama Cha Mapinduzi. But once he had been assured that it was strictly off-the-record, he became candid, almost gossipy, about a number of party leaders.

Earlier in the day, when I offered to bring him tea during a conference break, he turned me down, saying: "Let me do it myself; it is at times like these that I can act as a normal human being."

Julius Kambarage Nyerere, politician, born 1922; died October 14 1999.

What we can learn
from Tanzania's hidden socialist history

Selma James
The Guardian, **London, UK**
11 December 2014

As we celebrate the 53rd anniversary of Tanzania's independence this week and the publication of its hidden socialist history written by Ralph Ibbott, we can learn from what the great 1960s anti-colonial movements accomplished. The central question for every country after independence was: how, without capital or expertise, to lift themselves up from the imperial legacy of poverty and underdevelopment?

Julius Kambarage Nyerere, leader of Tanzania's independence movement and its first president, found a way. The first Tanzanian to get a UK degree, he had left his village for primary school aged 12. The village, and its women remained his political framework. "My father had 22 wives and I knew how hard they had to work and what they went through as women," he said.

Nyerere had seen the welfare state created to protect people from capitalism. Returning, he told Tanzanians that they had to reject exploitation of the many by the few. He proposed ujamaa: African socialism. In the village, all worked and all benefited. Decisions were made by consensus. He had "grown up in tribal socialism."

While traditional society was generally presumed to be backward, Nyerere saw its social and economic possibilities for overcoming backwardness. Rural people, 96% of the population, could adapt the communalism they already knew to modern needs and aspirations, thus bypassing capitalism. It was socialism without money, rooted in the native soil; a strategy for a poor but sovereign country determined to pull itself out of poverty and remain sovereign.

Two major problems had to be overcome for rural communal life to flower. The first was the subordination of women: Have we ever heard about women's subordination from a head of state? Even today his words are startling:

"It is impossible to deny that women did, and still do, more than their fair share of the work in the fields and in the homes. By virtue of their sex they suffered from inequalities which had nothing to do with their contribution to the family welfare."

"The truth is that in the villages the women work very hard. At times they work for 12 or 14 hours a day. They even work on Sundays and public holidays ... But the men in the villages ... are on leave for half their life." The second problem was tackling the poverty. This could be overcome, by updating agricultural methods. And if men pulled their weight, this "could contribute more towards the development of the country than anything we could get from rich nations."

Nyerere assumed that with ujamaa, people who had just won independence working communally, without bureaucratic interference, would themselves develop while resolving both problems.

Some people decided to put ujamaa into practice in 1960, even before Nyerere had invented the name for his bold and imaginative strategy. They succeeded brilliantly in Litowa, the first ujamaa village they created – organising production, distribution, housing, health and

130

education. Others came to join and were encouraged to form new villages; limiting village size enabled all to have a voice. When there were a few villages, the Ruvuma Development Association (RDA) was formed with its Social and Economic Revolutionary Army to help new villages to establish themselves. By 1969, the RDA had 17 villages.

A couple of times a week the village had communal meals where they made decisions. The women were encouraged to speak – a slow process – and their interests were considered. Housework and childcare counted as part of the village workday. Soon piped water ended fetching and carrying by women and children. Spare cash from sales of surplus crops was divided equally among all, including to elderly and disabled people who contributed by scaring wild animals from "sharing" food crops, or working in the new childcare facility.

Child mortality plummeted. Pupils at the self-governing Litowa school came from all the villages, boarding at Litowa in term time. They were not trained to compete or join the educated elite but to develop their exciting, caring rural society. Domestic violence virtually disappeared. Women's status was rising, and the disapproval of others was discipline enough.

Nyerere backed them. When people asked what he meant by ujamaa, he would send them to Ruvuma. Just as ujamaa was about to mushroom into a mass movement, the RDA was destroyed by the greedy and ambitious new ruling elite, capitalism by the back door. They, hated the creativity of the people which had Nyerere's support. Where was the power for them? Thus a great grassroots development, which might have changed the history of Tanzania and beyond,tragically ended. Nyerere, defeated, continued to work for socialist equity, in general and between the sexes.

By 1985, Tanzania had the highest primary school enrolment in sub-Saharan Africa – 96%; and girls made up

50% of pupils. Women's life expectancy increased from 41 years in 1960 to 50.7 in 1980. Maternal mortality dropped from 450 per 100,000 births in 1961 to under 200 in 1973. Ibbott returned to the UK and applied ujamaa principles as community development worker in Greenock, one of Glasgow's most deprived areas. The tenants' association and youth club persuaded the council to build a sports centre which the youth ran. Much was accomplished by young people previously dismissed as troublemakers. Such communal effort can succeed anywhere if it is able to bypass or defeat those greedy for power and control.

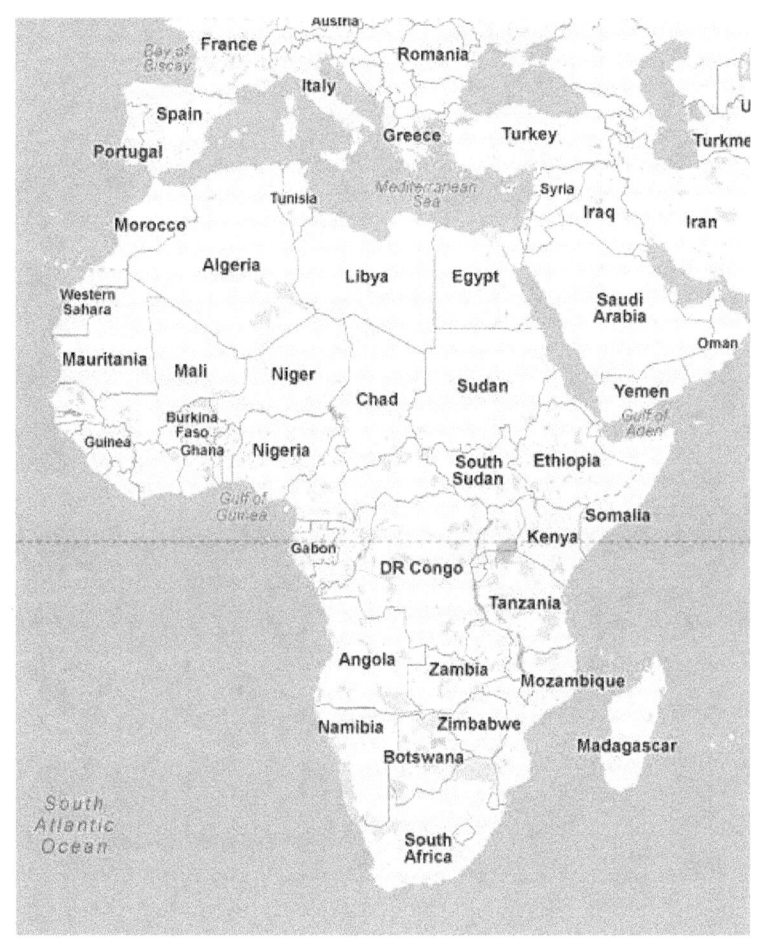